LET THEM

The Story
of a
Tibetan Buddhist Monk

Alice Herter

First Edition
Published 2023

Library of Congress Data:
Title: Let Them, The Story of a Tibetan Buddhist Monk/Alice E. Herter
Description: Biographical/Religious/Spiritual/Buddhism
Identifiers: ISBN# 979-8-9875888-0-2

*Some of the words and terms used
in this text may be unfamiliar
to the average reader.
Many of these words are
of Sanskrit and Tibetan origin.
For this reason, a Glossary of Terms
is included at the back of this text.*

TABLE OF CONTENTS

LAMA KARMA DORJE – SECRET YOGI

ACKNOWLEDGEMENTS:

Foreword

I am very happy Alice Herter has written a book about Very Venerable Lama Karma Dorje. She is a devoted student of his and has based her writing on her personal experience being around him. I believe that she was deeply inspired to write his life story so that others might be inspired by it as well.

I personally knew Lama Dorje as a child when I came to the monastery at the age of seven. I remember soon after I arrived, Lama Dorje entered the three-year retreat together with Bokar Rinpoche and several other monks. It was Bokar Rinpoche's second three-year retreat. I entered my own three-year retreat in 1979, the same year Lama Dorje was sent to Europe by our precious enlightened Guru, Kalu Rinpoche. From Europe, Lama Dorje was sent to the Los Angeles dharma center and subsequently ended up in Santa Fe as a permanent director of the KSK Tibetan Buddhist Center there. He has now been there for more than four decades.

Based on my own experiences, I have great respect for Lama Dorje. He is one of the finest people I have ever met in my life. He is endowed with true moral and ethical and spiritual principles. From the point of view of Buddha's teachings, he truly abides by the three levels of discipline: the monastics vows, the bodhisattva vows, and the tantric samaya vows. I can say without hesitation he is someone who upholds all these levels of discipline. For that, I have great respect for him.

When I myself was a young Buddhist teacher, struggling to represent my precious enlightened Guru and Buddhadharma, Lama Dorje was one of the very few people who really supported me and wished me well from the bottom of his heart. For that, I owe him eternal gratitude. Bardor Tulku Rinpoche from KTD Woodstock was also deeply moved by Lama Dorje's kind support and encouragement. When Lama Dorje was in a serious car accident, Bardor Tulku Rinpoche immediately came forward with his wish to help Lama Dorje by offering his blood if Lama Dorje needed a transfusion. His offer underscores his recognition of Lama Dorje's extraordinary qualities. When Lama Dorje was in this accident and later when he had a stroke, I immediately got my plane ticket and went to him and offered to help in any way that I could. He means that much to me. I was more than eager to volunteer.

I am sure that people who read this book will be inspired by Lama Dorje's extraordinary qualities. His qualities are truly genuine, noble spiritual qualities that I believe are coming from many past lives of spiritual training. There is a saying in the Buddhist tradition that "so and so" is truly a hidden Bodhisattva. I can say without qualification that truly, Lama Dorje is that hidden Bodhisattva. Even though he is not world-renowned, he is one of the finest beings on planet earth. I wish Lama Dorje longevity, health, happiness and spiritual well-being for the benefit of all his students.

I want to thank Alice Herter for her effort in writing this book for the benefit of everyone. I commend her for her intelligent observation of this noble being's extraordinary spiritual quality and wish her success in publishing this book. May all beings have happiness and the cause of happiness.

Sincerely,

Wangchen Rinpoche

November 26, 2022

SER CHO LING
626-688-0983
54333 Two Hills Rd
North Fork, CA 93643
http://sercholing.org

Preface

Writing a book about great and enlightened people is never an easy task. The task is made even more challenging by an ordinary being such as me, attempting to write about an extraordinary being such as Lama Karma Dorje. And, as Lama Dorje himself has asked me on numerous occasions, *"Why even write such a book?"* Certainly, there are already many fine books written by and about many fine people. How could one hope to benefit beings by adding to these many voluminous works?

My motivation comes from the teachings of the Buddha himself. It is said that the Buddha gave 84,000 teachings, any one of which, if followed diligently and consciously, would lead one to enlightenment. So why give 84,000 teachings if just one would suffice? And the answer that the Buddha gave was that there are many different beings, with many different understandings, qualities, and abilities. Some will be more inclined to follow a particular teaching and a particular path, while others will be drawn to a different approach. And if teachings are given to reach the greatest number of people in the greatest number of ways, then each of these 84,000 teachings becomes necessary.

I am also motivated by the desire to give the world heroes. So much of our culture worship today centers around people with temporary, often superficial qualities. Is our greatest aspiration as a people to be physically beautiful? Or flamboyantly wealthy? To drive expensive cars? Or attend lavish parties? I think most of us know deep down that these things are transient. And yet, whose lives fill the pages of magazines? Whose lives are the subject of television talk shows and morning coffee conversations? Hopefully, reading the lives of great contemporary beings will open our hearts and minds to other more meaningful heroes and deeper more lasting values.

Although many great books have been written about many great teachers, the story of Lama Karma Dorje has never been told. It is both a privilege and an honor to bring together and describe the many teachings and great accomplishments of an individual who has devoted his entire life to helping people. While most of us spend countless hours trying to make some semblance of worth out of our own individual lives, beings such as Lama Dorje take living their lives to a higher plain. The living of their own lives in a true and wholesome manner is merely the beginning step. They are committed to the higher purpose of helping **all** sentient beings live a meaningful and purposeful, enlightened life. In fact, one of the most basic and often recited Buddhist prayers says:

> *In the Buddha, his teaching, and the Order most excellent,*
> *I take my refuge until enlightenment is reached.*
> *By the merit of generosity and other good deeds,*
> *May I attain Buddhahood for the sake of all beings.*[1]

Lama Dorje does not give teachings in the more usual way. Often Buddhist teachers travel to various Buddhist Centers, advertising their arrival, and announcing the topics of their teachings. This is the more formal way of teaching and it is not without its own merit. Quite the contrary. Many students and practitioners, myself included, have benefited greatly from this more formal manner of teaching. I mention this only as a contrast to the way Lama Dorje gives teachings. As those fortunate enough to have received teachings from Lama Dorje know, Lama's teaching is simple and direct. He teaches in the moment, sometimes after meditation practice or from an activity in which he and his students may be engaged.

So, in compiling this book of Lama Dorje's teachings and accomplishments, it will also not follow the traditional format. Lama's teachings and accomplishments will be presented with a limited amount of narrative, trying as best as possible, to transmit his teachings in the concise and direct way that he gave them. Having worked with Western students for over forty years, Lama Dorje has a great understanding of the Western mind. He knows that we are unlikely to spend hours reading detailed treatises explaining Buddhist concepts. He also knows that we prefer talking about a thing rather than doing it! So, his teachings always go right to the heart of the matter, unobscured by clever language or debatable concepts.

---

[1] *This prayer is one of the most basic prayers that anyone on the Buddhist path takes. It is referred to as the "The Refuge Prayer of the Bodhisattva Path" or simply, the "Refuge Prayer." Bodhisattva is a Sanskrit word for the name of anyone who, motivated by great compassion, makes a commitment to attain Buddhahood for the benefit of all living things.*

I am still left with the necessity of providing some overall organization to this book. After much thought, I have organized this presentation around the so-called "*Six Perfections*" in Buddhism or "*Prajnaparamita*" as they are more traditionally called. I have chosen also to allow Lama Dorje's students to tell their stories and experiences in their own words with limited narrative or explanation from me. This direct sharing carries with it the unique flavor of each student as well as the backdrop in which Lama Dorje gave the teaching.

Throughout the text I use many Buddhist terms that may be unfamiliar to some readers. I recognize the difficulty of this because I myself had to learn an entirely new vocabulary as I began studying Tibetan Buddhism. So, in keeping with the tradition of many books about Tibetan Buddhism, I have included a Glossary of these terms at the end of the book.

I have also used the names of many people throughout the text. For the ease of reading and understanding, I have not always tried to identify or describe many of these people in the text itself. I have included a list of these people with the briefest of biographies about their relationship to Lama Dorje or to the topic of discussion in the Acknowledgements section at the conclusion of the book.

Finally, a word about the title of the book. As students of Lama Dorje know and learn, Lama is often a man of few words. He uses short, pithy statements to convey a teaching of deep understanding. Over time, these statements come to mean many things. Statements such as:

"Better than nothing"
"Maybe next time"
"People has kinds"
"Let them"

I have chosen to use one of these statements, "**Let Them**," as the title of this book. To me, this statement means a kind of letting go. When situations seem complicated or confused, when actions seem questionable or even wrong, when you are unsure about what to do or what your response should be, "**Let Them**" means a kind of turning things

3

over to the universe. Tibetan Buddhism embraces this in a practice called "*tong len.*" Christianity calls it turning things over to God. Support groups use the Serenity Prayer. The essence of all is the same, a recognition that not everything is within our control. Action is important, yet what is sometimes thought of as "*inaction*" is often the best choice. Letting go, recognizing our limitations, accepting those limitations and letting the situation play out in its greater picture is often the best approach and wisest advice.

Meeting Lama Dorje

I met Lama Dorje for the first time in the fall of 1989. At the time of that meeting, I was living in Santa Fe, New Mexico where I was an attorney and had been practicing law there since I moved to Santa Fe from Washington, D.C. in 1981. A friend of mine from northern New Mexico was living temporarily in an apartment complex across from the KSK Tibetan Buddhist Center in Santa Fe while she completed her studies in Nursing. She told me about meeting a Buddhist monk who had a Tibetan Buddhist Center where meditation practices were held. She said she wanted me to meet him. We arranged for me to come to one of the meditation sessions where she would introduce me. The monk was leading a meditation practice at 5:30 pm on Wednesday evenings. My friend suggested that I come to that meditation session which I said I would do.

Now 5:30 pm was an early time for me to leave work but I arranged my schedule so I could get to the meditation on time. The KSK Center was on the diagonally opposite side of the city from where I worked. Although I thought I was leaving in sufficient time to get to the Center by 5:30 pm, I had not accounted for the delays caused by commute traffic at that time of day. When I arrived at the Center, I was about 10 minutes late. I went to the door of the stupa where my friend said she would meet me, but there was no one there and the door into the meditation room was closed. I was uncertain about what to do. I did not want to enter the meditation room after the practice had started because I felt it might be disruptive to the folks who were meditating. I decided instead to just wait on a bench that was outside the door until the meditation was over and my friend emerged. I realize now that I could have gone in with minimal disruption but because I had never been to meditation at this center, I was cautious. I will admit that sitting and waiting was not

4

without its challenges as it was dark and cold and getting colder by the minute. I was not appropriately dressed for this nighttime winter weather as I had come straight from work and was wearing a dress, stockings and heels! I also had no idea about how long the practice would last. Finally, about an hour and a half later, my friend along with the Buddhist monk emerged. They were surprised to see me sitting there. I explained what I had done and the kind monk, Lama Karma Dorje, said, *"Well come in now and we will talk."* So along with my friend, we entered the stupa. I had never been inside this building and was awe struck as I walked in and saw the magnificent interior. The three of us sat on the floor and talked. I was so overcome by both the setting and the Lama that I have little recollection even today of what was said. However, I did remember quite clearly that Lama Dorje invited me to come back. He said, *"You are always welcome here."* I thought this was an extremely gracious thing for him to say to someone who arrived late without any idea of what to do!

And I did go back, and I learned what to do. Learning what to do may sound strange. Although I had many years of meditation experience in a more western, Christ-centered yoga, I had no experience with Tibetan Buddhist practice. In Tibetan Buddhist meditation, practitioners sit on the floor with their feet tucked under them in what is called the lotus position. In front of where one sits there is usually a small, low table on which the meditation text is rested. Except for brief periods during the practice, the meditation is not a silent meditation but is instead, the chanting of prayers. The prayers are contained in small books called *"pechas"*. Each page of the text contains three lines: 1) the first line is the prayer written in Tibetan letters, 2) the second line is the phonetical sound of each of the Tibetan words and, 3) the third line contains the English translation.[2] The words of these prayers are chanted together as a group, and they are often chanted to a tune. It is quite beautiful just to listen to the chanting even if you are unable to follow the words in the text.

At this initial meeting with Lama Dorje, he mentioned that the Center had a bookstore. The bookstore was closed for the day, but he suggested that I come back and see what might be helpful. Several days later, I did. At the bookstore I met Jean Greene,

---

[2] *I have included some sample pages from a Buddhist text in the Appendix to this book. You will notice the three lines of text referenced in the narrative above.*

the lady who ran the bookstore. She was very patient and very helpful. She told me that on the following weekend there was going to be a visiting Lama who was giving an "empowerment". I asked what this was and she explained that it was like an initiation into being able to do one of the Tibetan Buddhist practices. The visiting Lama was Lama Lodrö from a Tibetan Buddhist Center in San Francisco. The empowerment he was giving was Chenrezig. Chenrezig practice was and is one of the primary practices in Tibetan Buddhism and was the most often-used practice at the KSK Center.

I was intrigued. I was familiar with the writings of Alice Bailey of the Theosophical Society. In those books she talked often about "initiations" and how these were reserved for the highest of spiritual adepts. So the notion of actually seeing one happen, piqued my curiosity. But I was nervous about going to something like this by myself. I talked to my good friend Virginia and asked if she would go with me. Virginia seemed to have a better understanding of what to expect and she agreed to go. And we did. We received the empowerment for Chenrezig practice, not truly understanding exactly what that meant!

There was a young man there who had ridden to the Center on his bicycle. When the empowerment was over, he was looking for a ride back into town as it would have been quite cold riding his bike. We offered him a ride home. During that ride, he asked us who we had "taken refuge with". We looked at each other wide-eyed and said, "Refuge? What do you mean?" He explained that "refuge" was a vow and the first thing any Buddhist practitioner needed in order to do Buddhist practice. He said that usually you could not receive an empowerment until and unless you had taken refuge. Basically, as I later learned, Buddhists take refuge in what are called the "Three Jewels." They are 1) the Buddha, the fully enlightened one who is seen as a role model, 2) the Dharma, which is the teachings of the Buddha and, 3) the Sangha, the community of monks and nuns who have taken Buddhist vows. To take refuge in the Buddhist sense is to rest in the security that these Jewels can provide. The Three Jewels are a tangible and practical way to center ourselves in times of uncertainty and come back to the heart of our practice.

Virginia and I were interested in what we saw. I don't know if it was a genuine interest in the spiritual side of Buddhism or just downright curiosity. At that time, both

Virginia and I were members of and attended a local Episcopal church. Virginia was what they call a "cradle Episcopalian" meaning that she was an Episcopalian from birth. I was not. But the local church, St. Bede's, had a nice community of people which was quite meaningful. In addition, I had been a member for many years of a community near Taos, New Mexico, that followed the teachings of a spiritual leader named Herman Rednick. Herman's teachings were rooted in Christianity, Hinduism and Buddhism. Herman called it a "Christ-centered yoga", which is an accurate description. So, at the time that I met Lama Dorje, I had had some years of meditation practice and experience with Eastern religious beliefs as well as Christianity, the religion in which I was raised.

After meeting Lama Dorje, I knew I wanted to attend some meditation practices at the KSK Center and I did. As Lama Dorje had so graciously told me at our first meeting, I knew I was welcome to come back. Thus began my more than forty-year relationship with both Tibetan Buddhism and my teacher, Lama Karma Dorje.

THE BEGINNING

THE BEGINNING

The road was mostly hard-packed dirt with occasional sprigs of grass and weeds that showed a great desire to live in spite of numerous wheels and tires that had rolled over them again and again. The sky was slightly overcast, and the humidity hung heavy in the air like intangible raindrops. The temperature was hot and the air very still with the tension it gets just before the release of a heavy downpour. At that moment, there were no cars on the road or animals running loose. There was only one solitary monk walking softly and purposefully down the road. He wore flip-flops on his feet and he was wrapped in the beautiful burgundy red robes of Buddhist monks. He had on a saffron gold sleeveless shirt and his red stole (*tsen*) was draped partially over his head to protect him from the intensity of the sun still trying to break through the clouds. If you had been a constant companion of this road, you would probably find nothing unusual about that scene because that same monk had walked that same road wearing those same clothes many times before. Today was no different.

The monk had left his home high in the mountains of Sikkim and was on his way to visit his sister. As he walked, the monk suddenly heard the noise of sirens and the sound of a car coming down the road. The sound of sirens was not unusual on this road because it was a road often used by military officers and high government officials. As usual, the monk stepped off the road a slight bit in order to allow the car to pass. The car was coming faster than normal and as it approached it drove past the monk quite quickly. But only a few feet ahead, the car braked and came to a complete stop. At the same time, an arm draped in gold-colored cloth came out from one of the windows waving at the monk and telling him to come nearer. As the monk approached, the man inside the car said, "*I am on my way to have lunch at the palace of the Governor. After lunch, I will go back to Rumtek. You must come there to meet me because I have something special for you.*" The monk placed his hands together in salutation and nodded his head acknowledging that he would do as requested and immediately dropped to the ground and began doing prostrations.

The man in the car was His Holiness, the 16th Karmapa, leader of the Karma Kagyu sect of Tibetan Buddhism. The special thing he had was a passport. The passport was for the monk. And the monk was Lama Karma Dorje. And thus began the incredible journey and the beautiful story of a great man.

13

LAMA DORJE
A BRIEF BIOGRAPHY

LAMA DORJE

A Brief Biography

Lama Karma Dorje was born on May 25, 1933, in the town of Marchak in Sikkim. Sikkim is a small country bordered by Tibet to the north and east, Nepal to the west, Bhutan to the southeast and India to the south. Up until fairly recently, Sikkim was ruled by the Namgyal monarchy. According to legend, the Buddhist guru, Padmasambhava, visited Sikkim in the 8th century AD, introduced Buddhism and foretold the era of the Namgyal dynasty. With the Tibetan plateau rising from its northern border, Sikkim was part of the fabled Silk Road to China. In 1975, a referendum abolished the Sikkimese monarchy and the territory was merged with India.

Sikkim is the least populous state in India and the second smallest in size. But its tiny size, 2,740 square miles, belies its profound geographic diversity due to its location in the Himalayas. The climate ranges from subtropical to high alpine. Sikkim's geographical positioning has gifted it with a repository of over 5000 species of flowering plants including magnolias, poppies, geraniums, azaleas and camellias. Of the 5000 species of orchids known worldwide, 600 can be found in Sikkim, along with 30 different species of rhododendrons. The crowning glory of Sikkim is Mt. Kangchenjunga. At 28,208 feet it is the world's third-largest peak and the largest peak in India, located on Sikkim's border with Nepal. Due to a centuries-long population influx from Nepal, the majority of Sikkim's people today are of Nepali ethnic origin. However, the native Sikkimese were Bhutias, who migrated from the Kham district of Tibet. Today, the Tibetans reside mostly in the northern and eastern reaches of Sikkim and makeup only about 25% of its population.

Lama Dorje's parents were Tibetan. His mother's name was Kesay and his father was Rabgay Lama. Lama Dorje had four sisters and one brother. Lama Dorje was the oldest child. The family's religion was Tibetan Buddhism. Although a small state, Sikkim has over 75 Buddhist monasteries. Perhaps its most well-known monastery is Rumtek, the seat of the Karmapa, head of the Karma Kagyu sect of Tibetan Buddhism. And Rumtek is where Lama Dorje went to study art and to begin his monastic studies.

Lama Dorje entered monastic training when he was twelve years old and became a novice monk at the age of thirty at Sonada Monastery in Darjeeling. The decision of who would be sent to the monastery was often the decision of the head or chief official of the village. For the children who went there , the monastery was much like a school. The children were taught many subjects and as their training continued, if they showed interest and ability in a particular area, their training was gradually focused to that area. In the Sikkimese tradition, the children in the monastery went back to their villages every day and returned the next morning to continue their training. This was different from the Tibetan tradition where children who were accepted into the monastery stayed there and returned home only occasionally. Lama describes this process like this:

> *Sikkim is a small country with small villages. Just like Taos is a small village. Whoever is the head of the village decides who will go to the monastery. For example, like Albuquerque ... the Albuquerque mayor decides ... or in Taos, the Taos mayor decides. If that person says the children must go to the monastery, then children must go. Also, Sikkim tradition is a little different than the Tibetan tradition. In Tibet when the children go to the monastery, they stay. In Sikkim, they not always stay ... they go and come back ... go and come back. Maybe one time a year they stay when there is a celebration. Then they stay in monastery at that time.*

Even before he entered his monastery training, Lama was learning from his grandfather some of the Buddhist traditions. Lama says:

> *In beginning time, maybe I was 7 years old, my grandfather [my mother's father's brother] lived in our village and was a teacher there. He was always offering water ... seven bowl offering ... and he always prayer doing. We kids no understand but from small boy time we go and we watch him. We watching and we thinking, "What grandpa doing??*
> *We go and we watch and then he teach us the things in the seven bowl offerings ... argham, padyam, puphe, duphe, alokhe, gendhe, newidye, shabta [drinking water, washing water, flowers, incense, candle, rice, perfume, food, and music] ... He teach us these things. He sometimes used different names but the same meaning. And Grandpa*

18

say, "Now you learn and you no forget." And we only 7 years old but we learned and we no forget.

Lama Dorje was a smart boy and a quick learner. He did well in monastery. Lama Dorje was also a gifted artist. At the monastery, he began his training in thangka[3] painting. The training for thangka painters is quite different from the training in Western art schools. Thangka training takes anywhere from seven to eight years or even longer. Thangka painters, like painters in the West, must learn many of the mechanics of painting. They need to learn things like how to create various colors, what pigments to use, how to prepare the painting medium, what brushes to use, and so forth. In fact, they often make their own pigments by grinding certain stones into a very fine powder and when necessary, mixing those powdered stones to obtain the desired color. But in addition to learning the mechanics of painting, thangka painters must practice and study the various texts and meditations that relate to Buddhism. They must practice and recite daily the Buddhist texts that relate to the subjects of their paintings. They must acquire and gain a deep understanding of the subject itself. For example, if one wanted to do a painting of the Tibetan deity Green Tara, one would have to develop a deep understanding of who Tara was as well as an understanding of all the symbolic objects that she holds or creates. They would need to be deeply familiar with her origins and her purpose. And they would acquire this knowledge through regular, daily practice of the sacred Tibetan texts.

Perhaps the depth of the understanding that is required of Tibetan thangka painters could best be contrasted to a Western artist painting a floral landscape. Not only would the artist need to know the color and style of every flower in the composition but also acquire a deep understanding of how each petal of the flower is formed, how it travels from the seed placed in the ground into a small sapling, then how leaves develop and how the stamen and pistil of the flower are formed. They would also need to understand the life cycle of each plant and what it needs to grow and form and fulfill its purpose.

Because he was such a gifted artist, Lama Dorje completed the full thangka training in the monastery. He painted thangkas, sculpted deity figures and prepared sacred

---

[3] *A thangka is a Tibetan Buddhist painting often depicting a Buddhist deity, scene or mandala. Thangkas are usually painted on silk and mounted on a textile backing somewhat in the style of oriental scroll paintings.*

mandalas and mandala offerings. Lama also explained the taking of vows after this early monastic training:

> *Many teachers come and give teachings. Some people want to take vows and some people do not want to take vows. Each person decides what vows they want to take. Some no want to take vows but want wife and family and so they work and take care. Other people take vows and go to the gompa where they feed you breakfast, lunch and dinner. They take care of you in the gompa. So people eat the food and in the gompa stay. In the morning they serve you tea and tsampa (barley). In the evening they serve you Thukpa (soup) and then sometimes in between they give you tea, maybe three cups.*

After he completed his early training in the monastery, Lama Dorje left Rumtek and went to live high in the mountains with a teacher who Lama always referred to as "the 88-year-old Lama." He was a Sikkimese lama who Lama Dorje knew as a young boy. This Sikkimese lama had traveled back and forth to Tibet many times where he received special teachings. The 88-year-old lama had a house high in the Himalayas with a dramatic view of Mt. Everest. He lived a solitary life. Lama Dorje said he too preferred a solitary life to living in a monastery.

In addition to the main house, the 88-year-old lama had a small cabin on his property and he invited Lama to live there. Lama Dorje always describes the 88-year-old lama as very sturdy and strong. Lama Dorje tells a story of helping the 88-year-old lama build a fence. There was a large tree that had fallen and the 88-year-old lama wanted to use it for his fence. Lama Dorje tried to lift it by himself but could not do so. The 88-year-old lama came down and lifted one end of the tree onto his shoulder effortlessly. Lama Dorje then lifted the other end and together they moved the tree.

After several years of living with the 88-year-old lama, Lama Dorje began contemplating doing a three-year retreat. He wanted to do the retreat with the renowned lama called Kalu Rinpoche. He discussed his plans with the 88-year-old lama who told him he was very happy that Lama wanted to do this and said that if this was what he wanted, he should do it. But the 88-year-old lama also said, "*You must do this, but I will not be here when you return*". He told Lama Dorje that his home in the Himalayas would always be waiting for Lama's return and he was welcome to live there.

Lama Dorje came down from the mountain retreat and went to Sonada to speak with Kalu Rinpoche. Lama took everything he owned and sold it. He had a solid gold ring made and gave it to Kalu Rinpoche. Kalu Rinpoche invited Lama Dorje to do the three-year retreat with him. This retreat requires the monks to be completely removed from the world for three years, three months and three days without any contact with the "outside" world. About two years into the retreat, Lama Dorje one day had a revelation that his 88-year-old lama had passed away. His revelation was correct.

After he completed the retreat, Lama Dorje took his monk vows and received full ordination at Rumtek Monastery in Sikkim, the monastery of His Holiness Karmapa. Lama Dorje returned to the home that he had been given by the 88-year-old Lama. Lama loved the peacefulness of his retreat home and expected that he would spend the rest of his life there, but that was not to be. Lama was still a relatively young man in his forties. Both the Karmapa and Kalu Rinpoche wanted Lama to come to the West and assist the Tibetan Buddhist centers that were beginning to be established there. In 1980, His Eminence Kalu Rinpoche and His Holiness Karmapa requested that Lama Dorje visit various centers in Europe, including France, and also New York, Los Angeles and Seattle. So, Lama Dorje traveled with Kalu Rinpoche from India to France.

France

While in France, Kalu Rinpoche advised Lama Dorje that he wanted him to go to Los Angeles to assist a fledgling Center which was started by students and followers of Kalu Rinpoche. Although Lama Dorje had a passport, he had been unable to obtain a visa to the United States while he was still in India. A Western student of Kalu Rinpoche who was the mother of Trinlay Tulku[4], traveled to Calcutta to try to obtain a US visa for Lama Dorje but was unable to do so. So instead, she got a visa for Lama to France where her husband was a high official in the French government. Lama Dorje traveled to France with Kalu Rinpoche where he stayed at Rinpoche's retreat center in France.

---

[4] *Karma Trinlay Rinpoche is a highly accomplished Buddhist teacher and meditation master. He was born in 1975 to an American mother and a French father who served many years in the French Parliament. He was recognized as a young child, only 13 months old, by the 16th Gyalwa Karmapa as a reincarnation of an important Buddhist teacher. Rinpoche is the first Westerner to be recognized as a reincarnation of a high Buddhist teacher in the Karma Kagyu tradition of Vajrayana Buddhism.*

Lama Dorje stayed in France for about three months. While they were there, Kalu Rinpoche again tried to help Lama Dorje obtain a visa to the US. Rinpoche wrote a letter to his California Center and told them that he had a lama who he would send to Los Angeles to help the Center. He also told them that someone from the Center needed to come to France to pick up this Lama and accompany him to Los Angeles. They waited in France for about a month when an older man named Gerald Brill, a student of Kalu Rinpoche's from the Los Angeles Center, arrived to take Lama Dorje back to Los Angeles. When he arrived, Kalu Rinpoche asked him to help get a US Visa for Lama Dorje.

Brill traveled with Lama Dorje to Paris where Brill attempted to persuade the American Embassy in Paris to issue a visa for Lama Dorje. However, Brill and the embassy official had communication difficulties. He told Brill that there were already many Buddhist teachers in the US and wondered why one more was needed. He said there were already Buddhist teachers and monks from Vietnam, China, and Japan. Why did the US need another one? Brill argued that there were no teachers from Tibet but the embassy official remained unconvinced and refused to issue the visa.

After they returned from Paris, a second attempt was made to secure a US visa for Lama Dorje. Kalu Rinpoche wrote a letter to the American Embassy requesting a visa for Lama Dorje as a visitor to the US. This time was successful and Lama received his US Visa. Before leaving France, however, Gerald Brill wanted to take Lama Dorje to see the Eiffel Tower. It was a difficult trip. Brill spoke no French and people were unable and sometimes unwilling to help them find out train information. They claimed that they couldn't understand English and admonished him for not speaking French. But Brill and Lama persevered. They made it to the Eiffel Tower, went to the top and ordered food. Brill had great difficulty trying to order food and lost patience with the waiter who claimed not to understand him because he could not speak French. In the end, they wound up with only a glass of orange juice! Well, so much for French cuisine!

New York

New York, a city that welcomes over one hundred thousand immigrants each year, was Lama Dorje's first port of arrival in the U.S. He traveled from France and stayed at Lama Norlha's newly founded Center located in a high-rise skyscraper in downtown Manhattan. Lama Dorje's first impressions about New York were that it was a place of great noise and activity unlike anything he had ever witnessed. Remember, Lama was born and grew up in a village in the small country of Sikkim, the least populated and smallest state in India. That period of his life was followed by years in the monastery. Even when he traveled to France, he was staying in Kalu Rinpoche's retreat center, a place of quiet contemplation. Also, at that time, Lama Dorje spoke very little English. Although he had tried to learn some English before leaving India, his knowledge was limited to a few words with almost no experience in conversational-style English.

The original intent of the group traveling with Lama Dorje was to leave New York City and go to Lama Norlha's Center in Wappinger Falls. However, when they arrived, they learned that the His Holiness Karmapa was arriving in New York in the next few weeks, so they stayed to join the group welcoming the Karmapa. A large group gathered at the airport to celebrate the Karmapa's arrival. The Karmapa was going to Woodstock to Khenpo Karthar's Center. Along with the people who came from Woodstock, the people from Lama Norlha's center also wanted to follow the Karmapa to Woodstock. They gathered up their belongings at Lama Norlha's Center, climbed into waiting cars and drove together to Woodstock. There was only one problem. In the rush to make things appropriate and fitting for the Karmapa, no one had explained the plan to Lama Dorje. Remember again, that Lama Dorje spoke and understood very little English at this point in time. And as many of us know, Lama Dorje is an extremely humble man. He watched people climbing into cars as they left Lama Norlha's Center. But, as Lama Dorje describes it, *"No one invited me to get into one of the vehicles and join them."* He assumed that meant that they did not want him to go. In truth, knowing how quickly things move when distinguished teachers visit a Center, I doubt that their exclusion of Lama Dorje was intentional. More than likely, in the hustle and bustle, no one probably even noticed that Lama Dorje had not gotten into one of the cars. And Lama Dorje, being the humble and somewhat shy man that he is, would not impose himself into this group unless it was clear that he was welcomed to do so. Whatever the reason, Lama Dorje was truly left as the last man standing.

But all was not lost. A student of Lama Norlha's who was at the Center, noticed Lama Dorje and asked him why he had not gone with the group. Lama said he did not know where the group was going. Furthermore, he said that no one had invited him to go. This man recognized the problem. He asked Lama Dorje if he wanted to go to Woodstock where the Karmapa was going and Lama Dorje said that he would like to go. This man said he also would like to go and fortunately for them, he had a car. The man drove them to Woodstock where Lama Dorje joined the group.

When they arrived, however, the Karmapa and his attendants and the accompanying lamas had already been seated in the meditation hall. There was literally nowhere for Lama to sit. After a few minutes, Lama noticed that one of the attendants to the Karmapa kept "nodding off". He was sitting in the row immediately below the Karmapa. Because of the limited seating, Lama Norlha was sitting on the floor several rows down from the Karmapa. The attendant suddenly rose and walked away from his seat and out of the meditation hall. Then, to the consternation of some of the other Lamas, Lama Dorje walked over to the place the Karmapa's attendant had vacated and took a seat. Apparently, the Karmapa had watched this entire scene and started laughing when Lama Dorje took his seat in the row below him.

After the Karmapa's visit in Woodstock, Lama Dorje returned with the others to Lama Norlha's Center in Manhattan. Gerald Brill, Kalu Rinpoche's student from the Los Angeles Center, had arrived in New York and together with Lama Dorje, they flew to Los Angeles.

Los Angeles

Now imagine if you will what arriving in Los Angeles must have felt like for Lama Dorje. Here is a Tibetan monk, from the small country of Sikkim, having spent much of his early life in Buddhist monasteries, arriving in Los Angeles. Los Angeles is a city with a population in 1980, the year he arrived, of over 3 million people. Although Lama now speaks several different languages, at that point in time one of those languages was not English. So here he was arriving in a super-sized city of overwhelming proportions, unable to speak the native language. While composed of people with good and well-motivated intentions, the Center in Los Angeles at that time was quite loosely organized. In the early days, this was not necessarily an unusual thing among newly founded Tibetan Buddhist Centers in the west. And this was also the reason that Kalu Rinpoche wanted to send Lamas to these new centers so they could provide both direction and organization to the participants.

The stories of Lama Dorje in those early days in Los Angeles abound. While inquiring about those times, it was not easy to separate fact from fiction. In some instances what may have started out as fact became embellished over time. The telling of the event may have reached a somewhat mythical proportion.   But this is not necessarily bad nor even unusual. Most of history is ultimately recorded this way. Suffice it to say that in the recounting of these events, I have accepted both the truth and the wisdom of this story-telling process. One such event was the much-recounted tale that Lama Dorje was "the runaway Lama." Supposedly, Lama Dorje one day disappeared and no one from the center knew where he had gone. They were, of course, worried about him and based on their inability to find him or even perceive what was happening, they concluded that he had "run away." Acting out of their concern, they contacted Kalu Rinpoche and said that Lama Dorje had run away.

At about this same time that Lama Dorje was dispatched to Los Angeles, a three-year retreat at Kalu Rinpoche's Center in France was concluding. In this group of newly ordained Lamas was a woman named Sarah Harding. Sarah is an exceptional woman. She is one of the first western women to complete the three-year Lama retreat. Sarah had also studied and learned Tibetan and was fluent in both speaking and reading the language. When word reached Kalu Rinpoche in France that Lama Dorje had "run away," he asked Sarah to go immediately to Los Angeles to assist Lama Dorje. Sarah was the perfect choice. In addition to her spiritual training as a newly ordained Lama and her fluency in the Tibetan language, Sarah had actually grown up in Los Angeles and had some familiarity with that large and fast-growing city.

Another set of factors sheds some understanding on the so-called "runaway" event. When Kalu Rinpoche traveled from India to France, he brought with him not only Lama

Dorje, but several other Lamas that he intended to place in other western centers that were developing. Among them were Lama Rinchen, Lama Trinley Drugpa, and Lama Norlha, all of whom were known to Lama Dorje. It is not unlikely that Lama Dorje may have decided to travel to one of the other cities where Kalu Rinpoche Lamas had been dispatched. Bear in mind that these events occurred well before everyone carried cell phones in their pockets or had ready access to abundant digital information. If you were raised in a country where your primary mode of travel was your feet, you might also have tried to walk to find a friend. In addition, if you found yourself in a strange country where you could not even read the printed language that directional signs might offer, you may also have found yourself lost. [5] Little did Lama know or realize how far away the places of these other Lamas might be. You and I might be amused at someone suggesting that they were trying to walk from Los Angeles to San Francisco. But if you did not know the country, if you did not have access to any geographic information or even know how to acquire such knowledge in this strange country, you might have decided to take that same walking adventure!

Lama Dorje himself acknowledges that he was somewhat depressed in Los Angeles. The people at the Center were kind to him and brought him flowers, but the city

---

[5] *I had a not-so-different experience when I went to Japan in 1973. I arrived fully armed with a Berlitz phrasebook and maps of various cities in Japan. The day after I arrived in Tokyo, I went to the Japanese Travel Bureau (JTB) and they kindly and graciously helped me locate and reserve lodging for the month I was to be traveling in Japan. I wanted to stay in traditional Japanese lodging called ryokans rather than more western-like hotels. They also made reservations for me at a ryokan in Tokyo that they recommended. I had my luggage with me, and I told the JTB helper that I intended to go directly there after we finished. She had the wisdom and foresight to write out the name of the Ryokan and its address for me in Japanese to give to the taxi driver as she said otherwise, he would not be able to understand me. Her written directions were good and I arrived at this lovely and peaceful ryokan called the Bandiya Inn. I settled into my room and brought out my maps to begin to locate places I wanted to visit in Tokyo. The maps were lovely and contained much information except one thing was lacking: I did not know where on this map I was. I did not know the location of the Bandiya Inn. And, as you can imagine, a map becomes useless without knowing where you are on that map. I decided to go outside the Inn and look for street signs to gain my bearings. There were street signs on every corner but there was one major problem: The street signs were written in Japanese characters ... not anything was written with western-like alphabetical characters that I could read and recognize. For example, if you are traveling in Spain, you may not know what "Los Ramblas" means, but you can at least recognize the characters that the name is written in and find a match on the map. This was not possible when the names were written in Japanese characters. I made many attempts to explain my dilemma to the Innkeeper and his staff but they could not understand what I needed. So what did I decide to do? I decided to walk. I wanted to see if I could find some place of connection. I could not take a bus. I could not take a cab. Every mode of transportation required that either I know where I was going and certainly, that I knew an address of how to get back. Thus, I can well understand Lama's decision to walk to a place of connection on foot.*

itself was quite different. Lama says there was lots of smoke [smog] in the air and you couldn't open the windows. He said it was also very dirty and very noisy with police car sirens and helicopter noise all night long. The people from the Center tried to help. They took him to the beach, they took him to the mountains, and they took him to Santa Barbara. But even so, by his own admission, Lama was depressed and wanted to go back to Sikkim … he didn't want to live in Los Angeles … he wanted to go back to India.

One of the first things that was arranged for Lama Dorje after he arrived in Los Angeles was enrolling him in an English learning class at UCLA. A man named Tony Leitner organized a fund-raiser to acquire the funds to send Lama Dorje to UCLA. They raised almost $1000 dollars from this effort. The first time he went to UCLA for his English classes, Sarah Harding took him. Lama describes that event:

> *They made one thousand dollars for me to go to school to learn English. First, Sarah she take me with her small baby. She show me which bus to take and what time to go. She also show me which bus to take and what time to go stand at the bus stop to get back to the Center. But first time she showed me. In the evening, I took the 3 o'clock bus to go back. This kind of thing she did for me in the beginning. She teach me. Then after first time, I went by myself.*

> *Then English I learn. Writing I am no good but little bit of talking OK. They show you pictures of things and tell you to name what they are called … apple … motorcycle … bicycle. Then they ask you what the bicycle is doing … the bicycle is arriving …. Or the bicycle is leaving. That is how we learned it. At first I little bit baby talk … but little by little I learn it. That is how they teach us. They show picture and we name it and we must match the picture to the word. Good learning.*

There is one version of Lama Dorje's early adventures in Los Angeles that I actually heard him talk about. Lama learned which buses he needed to take to get to UCLA for his classes and which buses returned him home to the center. While at the center, Lama did meet a few people who came to do meditation practice. One of those people was a Tibetan man who lived in Claremont, California. Claremont is a suburban city on the eastern edge of Los Angeles County, 30 miles east of downtown. It has a population of about 35,000 people. The Tibetan man befriended Lama Dorje and would come to the center to visit with Lama from time to time. As he was taking the buses to his English classes at UCLA, Lama Dorje noticed several buses that said "Claremont" on the front of the bus. The Center itself was located in Pasadena. One day, Lama decided to go on his own and visit his friend in Claremont. So, in an adventuresome spirit, he hopped on one of the buses marked Pasadena because his friend said that Claremont was near Pasadena. He rode the bus waiting for it to arrive in Claremont. Lama's expectation was that Pasadena was a small little town with a small population where anyone would be able to direct him to his friend's house. Well, in fact, Pasadena is a Los Angeles suburb located about 11 miles northeast of downtown LA. It is, in fact, the 9th largest city in Los Angeles County. But having boarded a "Pasadena" bus, Lama could never figure out where to get off the bus to get to his friend's home. Speaking very little English, he also could not ask for help. So, Lama continued riding on the bus for many hours hoping that he would see something familiar and that the bus would eventually return him to his home center. He rode the bus late into the night until the time that the bus driver ended his route and returned the bus to the bus station. He explained to Lama Dorje that he had to get off the bus. Imagine for a moment, how both the bus driver and Lama Dorje were feeling. Here was a crusty, but kindly old bus driver, tired and glad to be finishing his route and going home, trying to help this monk in his red and saffron colored monk's robes, speaking no English.

Lama wanted to sleep in the bus station but they would not let him stay inside. He walked back out to the street and saw a man sitting on the sidewalk in dirty, shabby clothes. Lama asked him if he could go to his house and spend the night. The man said he could not do that. Then Lama asked him if he would take him to the police station. The man got quite agitated and told Lama "No! No! I cannot go to the police station because they will arrest me and beat me." But the man pointed out to Lama a hotel that was just down the street from the bus station where he could get a room for the night. Lama says:

> I want to sleep inside bus station but police they tell me no. Then I see man sitting outside bus station and I say to him I don't know where to go. Where can I stay? I say take me to your place please and I spend the night. He say, No ... my place a long way away. Then he say I tell you where to go and he point to hotel like place and he say you go. Then I go over to hotel. I say cheap hotel give me for 1 night. But no cheap. $30 for one night. I paid $30 then people very surprised that I could pay this

money. But me, I no understand. They show me room ... with two beds ... but then I see mice crawling into corner of bed. Then this room I occupied. I money paid. In early early morning I wake up and I want to go but gate out of hotel is locked. They no open the gate until 8 o'clock and then people could go out. Then I go back to my room to wait until 8 o'clock and they let me go.

Lama returned to the bus station. There was a policeman there. Of course, the policeman was in the same position as the bus driver the night before ... Lama could not speak English and the policeman could not speak Tibetan. Remember also, that this was in 1981, a time before people traveled with cell phones, so Lama had no way to call the center for assistance. Befuddled, and quite naturally so, the policeman decided to contact the FBI. The FBI picked Lama up at the bus station and took him to their offices. Lama describes that time as follows:

I again go to the bus station. I ask them please help me get back to my center in Pasadena. But Pasadena a big city and they ask me West Pasadena? East Pasadena? North Pasadena? But I don't know ... I have no telephone to call anyone and ask. Then I see bus that says Pasadena and I ask the bus driver. But I no have an address and I no have a telephone number. Then I ask them where is the police station. I tell them that I was lost. I tell them I cannot find my center.

The driver no want to take me there but he pointed out to me which way I should go. So I go to police station. I tell them I am lost. I tell them I no have address or telephone number. The police say they are going to take me to the FBI place. At the FBI place I am sitting across the desk from an Asian woman. She very kind. She ask me if I have had anything to eat. I tell her I no eat since yesterday morning. She tell me to wait and she will be back. She came back with a hamburger, an apple and a 7-up drink. I no really hungry but I am afraid if I don't eat this food she will get upset with me. So I eat.

Then more sitting. Then they take me to big room with lots and lots of people ... many nationalities ... mostly Chinese, Japanese and Vietnamese people. Then one older Anglo man come over and he ask me what happened? I try to tell him and he want to check my identity. I show him my passport and visa. Then I show him my money bag. I have 100 dollars that I had changed in India for India money to American money. He tell me you no show this to people here or they will kill you and steal it. He give me good advice. They kill you he say. I say OK. I will not show.

Again, no one there spoke Tibetan and Lama spoke no English. Then, as the story goes, the FBI contacted the CIA who apparently had someone who could speak Tibetan or Hindi, languages that Lama Dorje understood and could speak. The CIA was able to return Lama Dorje to his home center. And to this day, Lama Dorje has an almost reverential attitude about the CIA. Whenever he hears something on the news about the CIA, he says, *"Very good. Very good the CIA."*

Another story about Lama Dorje during his early days in this country occurred several months after Lama had arrived in LA. Before leaving Sikkim, many people warned Lama Dorje about the different foods that he would have to eat in the United States. One of the warnings was especially dire. They told him that people in the US did not eat white rice so he would have to get accustomed to eating other foods besides rice. This was a big change for Lama because rice was a daily staple in his diet. Now Lama was and is to this day a very good and very creative cook. People at the center in LA would go to the store for Lama and bring back food for him to prepare. He cooked whatever they brought without question or complaint. So for many months after his arrival in LA, Lama did not eat rice. He ate no rice and cooked no rice because he never requested it. He never requested it because he had been told and believed it to be true that there was no white rice in America. One day, as someone from the center was going to the grocery store to shop, Lama asked to go along. He had a natural curiosity and he wanted to see what these big grocery stores looked like inside. Imagine his amazement as he walked down one of the grocery aisles and discovered shelves and shelves of white RICE! There was more rice than he could ever have imagined existed anywhere! So our dear Lama was once again able to cook and eat rice.

Sifting fact from fiction about Lama's early days in Los Angeles may always be a fluid exercise, however, one thing seems to be clear. Los Angeles was not a good fit for anyone connected with the Center in those days. Sarah Harding describes those times in this way:

Our time in Los Angeles was pretty chaotic. The Center in Pasadena was not located in a very good area ... in fact, the area was pretty grim. Lama Dorje was a quiet and humble man, not particularly experienced in worldly ways. It was clear that he was not happy. He wanted to go home. I was not happy. Although I had grown up in Los Angeles, I never liked the city ... I never liked the smog.

Then, shortly after I arrived in Los Angeles, His Holiness Karmapa came to Los Angeles. Lama Dorje and I had an audience with His Holiness. His Holiness was a pretty intense man. He did not mess around. He got straight to the point, asking Lama Dorje directly, "What happened?" "What did you do?" . (Apparently, someone had told the Karmapa that the police had "picked up" Lama Dorje.) Lama Dorje was horrified. Then His Holiness started in on me asking, "Are you a nun?" "What vows have you taken?" I explained that I had taken the vows of a lay person. He just looked at me and said, "Poor thing." So, things in LA were not going well.

Kalu Rinpoche had said there were three places that had requested lamas: Los Angeles, Hawaii and New Mexico. I thought Lama Dorje might do better in a smaller place so I told Kalu Rinpoche that I thought we should go to New Mexico. So, we went there to visit. When we returned to LA, I told Lama Dorje that I thought Santa Fe would be a better fit. We went back to New Mexico for a second visit ... only this time, they did not give us a return ticket to LA. So, we stayed.

Lama Dorje describes the Los Angeles Center this way:

The center was there before I came. It was a two-story house ... a very good house ... but on the first floor area there were lots of liquor bottles. I saw that and I no go there. Top story OK but bottom not so nice.

The land was almost one acre. Big land with lots of flowers ... big red flower bushes ... almost jungle-like. Many flowers and orange orchard ... maybe three or four orange trees on center property. And there was one big palm tree. It was a new tree ... teenager-like tree. Very beautiful.

I would sit and look out at the trees and this one day a bird ... a black bird ... the size of a blue jay ... came to where I was sitting. Then one day I saw this black bird in the palm tree. He was sitting there and making all kinds of noise. He would fly away and then come back. Many many times I watch him. But then I make contact with him ... eyeball to eyeball. And then he be watching me and I be watching him.

One day I go over to this house that had volcano stone in it and one stone looked exactly like the black bird's head. And I think ...Amazing! It look just like him and then I know that this black bird go over there. So I brought the stone back. It had no eye on the stone but everything else the same as the black bird.

I keep that stone and I brought it with me to Santa Fe. But I no want to put in Santa Fe stupa. Many years later, when Norbert and I start building the stupa in Tres Orejas and then I put bird stone in Taos stupa. It no have any money value, but it have special value for me. And now up in Tres Orejas, when we have practice, many, many black birds come and we feed them.

Even though there were challenges at the Los Angeles Center, Lama always speaks very fondly of the people there. He says they were always very good and very kind to him.

Santa Fe

By all accounts, those early days in Los Angeles were challenging. Although the people there were kind and appreciated Lama Dorje, the circumstances surrounding the center were difficult. Like many other spiritually trained people, Lama Dorje has an uncanny ability to adapt to any situation. I have seen him poised and confident when the Dalai Lama and his entourage visited Santa Fe and equally comfortable talking with street beggars fully loaded with alcoholic spirits. But there seemed to be general agreement that Lama was not happy in Los Angeles.

Around this same time, there was a small group of people in Santa Fe who were followers of Kalu Rinpoche, trying to start a Tibetan Buddhist Center there. Some of those people, like Ken and Sally Maynard, Joan Lauber and others requested that Kalu Rinpoche send a Lama to Santa Fe to help them. The timing was right and Kalu Rinpoche decided to send Lama Dorje. He also asked Sarah Harding to go to Santa Fe as well, to help Lama Dorje make the transition to this new environ. So, in 1981, Lama Dorje arrived in Santa Fe. Sarah Harding also moved to Santa Fe to translate and assist Lama Dorje. By this time, Sarah was pregnant with her second child.

In those early days, Lama Dorje stayed with Ken and Sally Maynard at their home on Irvine Street in Santa Fe. Their home was also the place where the small group of

Buddhist practitioners held their meditation practice. They began looking for a place to establish a Center. A real estate agent who was a friend of some of the practitioners, found them land on Airport Road and, thanks to generous contributions, they were able to make a down payment on the land. They immediately started trying to repair some of the old adobe buildings located on the property to provide housing for Lama Dorje as well as a room where meditation practice could be held. About this time, Sarah gave birth to her son Sam. Sarah tells a very sweet story of this time:

> When I gave birth to Sam, my son and my second child, Heinrich and I were not yet living at the newly-acquired property on Airport Road. We were still living downtown in Santa Fe. Much to my surprise, Lama Dorje came to see me and the new baby. I asked him "Lama, how did you get here?" He said he had walked. The distance from the Center out on Airport Road to where we were living in town was about 17 miles round trip! I was deeply touched that he had made such a journey on foot to come to see me and the new baby.

Not long after this, Sarah and her family moved out from downtown Santa Fe to the KSK Center on Airport Road. They lived there eight more years. Sarah's children, Shana and Sam, thought of Lama Dorje as part of their family, and rightly so. Sarah says:

> Lama Dorje became a part of my children's family. He was like their uncle. Even today, they still see him that way. They go to visit and Lama always asks me about them and how they are doing. It is really very sweet.

Anyone who has had the opportunity to see Lama Dorje with children knows how special that relationship is. I remember one particular story about Sam, Sarah's son. He was little more than a toddler, probably about 4 or 5 years old with a cute little round face and curly blond hair. From time to time Sam would "sneak" away from home and go over and visit Lama Dorje. Bear in mind, that this sneak-away journey was never far because Lama's little house was really just on the other side of a small yard from the house where Sarah and her family lived. On these journeys to visit, Lama always had some kind of treat for Sam, often a nice little piece of chocolate candy that someone may have given him.

As most mothers do, Sarah tried to limit her children's intake of sugar. Also, as an observant mother, she soon became wise to the fact that Lama was giving Sam chocolate treats. She also noticed that Sam's visits to Lama were becoming more and more frequent resulting in a little game between Sam and Lama Dorje where Lama started calling Sam "Mr. Chocolate." Sarah told Lama that he should stop giving Sam chocolate candy. Lama listened but proceeded to give chocolate candy to Sam anyway. So, Sarah had a strong talk with Sam. She told him that if Lama gave him chocolate candy, he needed to tell Lama he could not take the candy because he was not allowed to eat it. Days passed until the day came when Sam could resist no longer. Once again, he wandered over to Lama's house. As Lama greeted him, Sam had a very sad expression on his face. Lama asked him what was wrong. Sam started shaking his head from side to side, looking close to tears, and said to Lama, *"No more Mr. Chocolate, Lama. No more Mr. Chocolate."* Lama loved telling this story about Sam and often used it as a basis for a lesson after meditation practice. The lesson was a reminder that we can't always get what we want. Boundaries exist, even if we do not like them or want them.

After Lama Dorje moved to the Airport Road property, Jerry Morell, a student of Kalu Rinpoche's and a long-time friend of Sarah Harding, arrived in Santa Fe. Jerry was a man of courage and ambition. With very little prior experience in construction, he had built the retreat center in France for Kalu Rinpoche. Applying that same "can do" attitude in Santa Fe, he told Lama Dorje that with Lama's direction, he would build a stupa at the Center in Santa Fe. And that is precisely what happened. With the help and generosity of many people, a stupa 65 feet tall was built on Airport Road. For those who are unfamiliar with this area, be aware that in the early days of 1981, Airport Road was a narrow two-lane road on the far southwest side of Santa Fe that took you out to Santa Fe's small, non-commercial airport. Today Airport Road is five lanes across and host to scores of homes, apartment complexes, stores, and gas stations. It is certainly no longer the sparse and secluded area it once was.

From a challenging beginning, Lama Dorje settled into Santa Fe. He has now lived there for almost 45 years. And, as you will continue to read, these years have been filled with intense activity that always reflected the strength of Lama Dorje's commitment to a path of kindness and compassion and a deep desire to help all sentient beings.

**LAMA DORJE IN HIS YOUNGER DAYS –
STILL SMILING TODAY AT 90 YEARS OF AGE**

LAMA DORJE MASTER OF THE DHARMA

LAMA KARMA DORJE

Master of the Dharma

The Teacher

From the moment we enter this world until the time we depart, we are continually engaged in learning. Some learn fast, others more slowly. Some quickly grasp certain subjects while other subjects remain elusive. But learning itself is a continuous process whether it comes quickly or tediously, or even ever. Certainly, many situations in life present teachers and lessons. It is sometimes said that our enemies can be our greatest teachers. Someone who continually criticizes what we say or what we do immediately feels to us like our enemy. We question their right to make negative statements about us and feel compelled to argue to set the record straight. Yet, on a deeper level, their criticism affords us the opportunity to examine our thoughts and actions and learn how we might be more skillful in the future. The enemy literally keeps us on our toes! And, as Carl Jung once exclaimed, *"Perhaps I myself am the enemy who must be loved!"*

The spiritual journey is not a matter of happenstance, even though it may sometimes seem that way. The spiritual journey requires a roadmap, a guide or a teacher who has traveled the path before you, someone who can help you understand the obstacles you face or help you determine which paths to follow and which to leave behind. Although we often pride ourselves on being independent and making our own way in the world, this is often a delusion, and sometimes a dangerous one at that. As the author Ray Bradbury once said, *"Sometimes I think I understand everything ... and then I regain consciousness!"*

In the spiritual practice of Buddhism, a basic tenet and most essential tool is having a spiritual teacher. Finding a true and authentic teacher is, in itself, a challenge. Teachers possess many different qualities that run the gamut from strict disciplinarian to "just one of the crowd." In seeking a teacher, we must listen to our heart and we must look at ourselves with honesty. As Jack Kornfield says in his book, *The Path With Heart*[6], "*the purpose of a teacher is to guide and protect us and create a space where our hearts and our spirit can open and blossom.*"

Lama Karma Dorje is such a teacher. But while the subject of finding a teacher is much discussed in many great books of and about Buddhism, one important factor about finding a teacher is sometimes overlooked. That fact is that the teacher must also accept you as a student. This is very much the case with Lama Dorje. Although he offers teachings freely and happily to all, he accepts students with what might be called "studied reluctance." Over many years he has watched students listen to a teacher, take empowerments with that teacher and make numerous vows propelled by the momentary excitement that can come in the presence of great and learned beings. Then, as the excitement dwindles, so do the vows and the commitments. Lama Dorje rarely, if ever, discusses his own qualities as a teacher or an enlightened being. Instead, he remains humble and unassuming; so much so that to some people for many years, he was thought to be merely the "caretaker" for the Buddhist temple and stupa. Many claimed he never gave teachings. Still others criticized him because he never gave "empowerments." And yet, those of us who were fortunate enough to be his students, know without doubt his remarkable teaching, not only in words, but in his every action. He never waivers from his vows and joyfully and steadfastly manifests the true Dharma in every action in his life. Just being in his presence makes you want to be the best that you can be!

One of Lama's students described him as follows:

> *Lama Dorje is a totally dedicated and endlessly principled exemplar of wisdom and compassion. He happens to be a devoted Buddhist practitioner, but his decency and ethics are not bound to any one religion. He understands human nature. Depending on what is most*

---

[6] *In his book, The Path of Heart, Jack Kornfield describes quite beautifully the qualities of a true teacher.*

beneficial, he will give precise directions or he will prod one to make the discoveries on one's own.

-   Rachel S.

Many who know Lama Dorje share this succinct description of him. One of his youngest students had the following to say about Lama Dorje:

I have known Lama Dorje since I was about 12 years old and he means the world to me. I grew up with very little extended family. Lama always seemed to be like all my grandparents combined. I remember many summer afternoons and evenings, sitting on the porch with Lama drinking tea. Lama said, "If you don't offer tea, people will say you have no hospitality!" So he always offered tea. We would sit on the porch talking. Lama talked about things that were not always serious Dharma. He always wanted to hear about my job or talk about things going on in the world, and yes, sometimes even a little friendly gossip! To be honest, these are some of the happiest memories of my life ... sitting on the porch with Lama.

-Will F.

For many years, I had the opportunity to assist Lama Dorje with his personal finances. Until recent years, Lama refused any salary from the KSK Center. He subsisted solely on donations given to him. And even with those donations, Lama turned every penny he received in donations back into Dharma activity. For example, in wintertime it can get quite cold in Santa Fe. If someone had given Lama a warm coat or jacket, he would wear it. If he had no such gift, he walked in the cold with only his short-sleeved monk's robes. Early in my acquaintance with Lama, I remember seeing him walk from his Lama hut to the stupa for meditation wearing flip-flops through the snow. It so impressed me that I was moved to buy shoes for him. He accepted the shoes and thanked me. But when I bought him a second pair, he thanked me and then quietly give them away to someone he felt more needy than himself.

If someone gave him food, he fixed it for himself and others and enjoyed it. If no such food was forthcoming, he subsisted on a bowl of rice. Yet, whenever someone came to visit Lama, he always offered them tea and food. His food supply reminded me of the long-told story of the woman in Biblical times whose family was experiencing severe poverty. The woman had stretched her food wisely to feed her family but the day came when all the food was gone except for a small amount of flour which she could use to make a loaf of bread. A stranger came by who was needy and quite hungry. The woman felt conflicted. What should she do? Should she use her last flour to make some nourishment for this man or should she keep the flour to feed her family? As the story goes, she used the last of her flour to make bread for this hungry stranger even though it meant that her flour bin was now completely empty. But miraculously, in the days that followed, her flour bin was always filled. Never again would she run out of flour to feed her family.[7]

Well, Lama's food supply was somewhat like that. Although his refrigerator was often quite empty, he somehow always managed to have enough to feed folks. He fed not only those who came to visit but any workers who were around the Center from time to time doing repairs. Lama was a good cook and the food he prepared was always very tasty. But in his never-ending ability to use all life experiences as an opportunity to teach, he used these food offering moments to demonstrate some Dharmic principle. When I met Lama Dorje I was a vegetarian and had been for a number of years. Lama knew this about me as I continued to maintain my vegetarian practice after meeting him. Even today the issue of meat-eating or non-meat-eating is a continuous matter of debate within the Buddhist community. And I suppose on some level, I may have felt a bit of self-righteousness about being a vegetarian so that no living creature had to die in order to feed me.

One busy day, I was returning to Santa Fe from Albuquerque. After a series of meetings, I had stopped at the oriental market in Albuquerque to pick up a few things that I knew Lama liked ... things like bitter melon and mustard greens and, of course, rice ... in a special Japanese-type that Lama seemed to prefer. Although I was rushing back to Santa Fe for yet another meeting, I stopped by the Center to leave these food items with Lama. He invited me into his little hut and told me to sit down. This was about two o'clock in the afternoon. He said, *"You have not had lunch, have you?"* I acknowledged that he was correct, I had not had lunch that day. He proceeded to fix me lunch. The lunch consisted

---

[7] *1 Kings 17:7 – 16 Bible, New International Version*

of one large Momo [Tibetan pot sticker].   As soon as I tasted the Momo, I knew it was made with meat. I was unsure what to do. I said to Lama, *"You know I don't eat meat, right?"* He said *"Yes. I know that."* I said, *"Well, I think this Momo contains meat, doesn't it?"* He said, *"Yes, it does. But it be OK."*   And in that moment, something happened. I saw my attachment to being a vegetarian for what it was … a bit of self-righteousness … as if the merit from that alone would get me into "Heaven." I ate the Momo. And I tell you truly, it was one of the most delicious pieces of food I have ever eaten. And believe me, I am not a timid eater!!

Another vegetarian student of Lama's tells of a similar encounter:

I was attached to being a vegetarian, having been one for 28 years. Lama enjoys meat but he doesn't enjoy attachment. Before I moved to Santa Fe to study with him, I periodically came to visit. On one visit I spent several days behind his house gilding tsa-tsa that were to be placed in the stupa being built in El Rito. Lama made a delicious vegetarian lunch for me every day. One day I asked about an ingredient and he told me it was tofu. I was suspicious because it had striations. But of course, I ate what was prepared. And of course, it was not tofu! Later as he talked about it, he gleefully exclaimed, "It be Poke [pork]! It be poke!" Eventually, I began to understand my attachment and ate some meat during an evening tsok [food offering]. I proudly told Lama and he said, "Good. Good. Now you eat menudo [tripe]!" Ugh. I did not. But I did start eating and enjoying meat.

-   Rachel S.

Here is yet another example of Lama using food as teaching tool:

In 1995 our little print shop which we had run for eight years went out of business. Soon afterwards, my husband Steve and I visited Lama Dorje in Santa Fe. The stupa in Lorien was nearing completion and we spoke about that some. Lama was very focused on Steve, telling him not to be sad because the business had gone under. These things happen, he seemed to say. Indeed, with the advent of quality computer printers, we felt fortunate to be able even to sell our used offset printing equipment. Then suddenly, the conversation switched to food! Lama described with great delight that we were now in for the deliciousness of poor people's food. He said we no longer had to eat the small, odd-tasting servings of strange food that rich people eat. We could just eat beans and chili and potatoes and good-tasting corn! How many times did I reflect on how right Lama had been? One can hardly feel deprived when eating large, smothered burritos, Spanish rice and papas y chili. And during that period of our lives, I never did miss the small servings of strangely prepared, supposedly exotic vegetables. I felt fortunate to be enjoying our hot, good tasting and wholesome food!

-Anna and Steve R.

A true spiritual teacher is a special gift. That teacher is not necessarily one who showers you with glowing praise and constant flattery. No. Compliments may please your ego but they do not necessarily contribute to your spiritual growth. A true spiritual teacher is not concerned with stroking your ego but with your spiritual development. Sometimes this means being confronted with your limitations or shortcomings. And who among us likes having these "failings" pointed out? But this is part of the job of a true teacher. And a true teacher has the wisdom and skill to point out our inadequacies while at the same time leaving our ego sufficiently intact to learn and understand the antidote for those actions. Many times our inadequacies result from our own lack of skill. Sometimes actions which we call "wrong" are actually mostly just "unskillful." Take, for example, the old adage often applied to children to "count to 10" before expressing their anger. A true spiritual teacher leads us on that "count to 10" journey. A true teacher shows us corrective action for our apparent mistakes. This takes a wise and compassionate teacher. This is Lama Karma Dorje.

VERY VENERABLE KALU RINPOCHE, LAMA
DORJE'S TEACHER AND RETREAT MASTER

LAMA KARMA DORJE
Master of the Dharma

The Teachings

Over many years, Lama has given literally thousands of teachings, certainly too many to summarize in this text. The challenge in recording his teachings becomes how to condense and format some of the teachings in a way that would be of some benefit to the reader. At the same time, as much as possible, the teachings should carry some of the flavor and spirit with which they were given. I have chosen two methods to try to accomplish this.

First, and I think perhaps the most meaningful, is to record the various stories and testimonials of his students themselves. Lama Dorje is such a skillful teacher that each of his teachings, though apparently similar in context, is often delivered in a different form depending upon the student. For example, Lama might say to a student, "You must think about marriage." One student might interpret this instruction as a direction to get married. Still another student might give the instruction a totally opposite meaning and say, "Lama told me never to marry." So, learning about Lama's teaching directly from the students themselves is perhaps the purest form. One of Lama Dorje's students described it well. He said:

> *Describing Lama's teaching style sounds kind of crazy. On the one hand, he never gave "formal" teachings. He never just announced that on Sunday night he was giving a teaching on Chenrezig, for example. And yet, he gave teachings on Chenrezig all the time. He gave teachings when people were ready and it didn't matter what we were doing. For example, we might be working on a building and maybe you were trying to find a hammer or something and suddenly Lama would be telling you something meaningful ... something really important. I mean he gave us teachings like this all the time. And it would happen quite naturally. It was kind of like when you are working construction with people, you get to know them in a different way. You get to know how they handle frustrations ... you get to know how they act when they make a mistake ...*

and it is all just part of the process. When you are working side by side, you aren't always thinking about the words you're using or the mood that you're in ... you just say things ... straight ... without always filtering them. Well, this was kind of the way it was with Lama. You are working on a building together and all of a sudden he is telling you something really important ... some dharma lesson or dharma truth. And sometimes other people working with you heard the lesson and got it and sometimes they didn't. Sometimes Lama would even tell the lesson in such a way that you knew it was meant directly for you. At the same time, not everyone there with you heard the same lesson. I do not know how he did it, but he could be talking to two different people, giving them two different teachings, at the same time.

And then there were times when he would give you a teaching in public when other people were around and maybe having a different conversation. It was like things were happening on two levels at once. I mean I was hearing a certain thing ... usually something I needed to hear ... while someone else was hearing something completely different. I don't understand how it was happening. His English is somewhat different. He knows English very well and he knows exactly what he is saying. But then sometimes when he talks, he talks in a way that you might think he does not understand English at all. But if you know him a bit ... if you have been around him and worked with him, you know exactly what he is saying. It is almost like he is speaking on two levels at once so that you hear what he wants you to hear while someone else may hear something different. I can't really explain it, but I know it happens because it happens to me. I have experienced it!

- *David B.*

In addition to sharing the experiences students have of Lama Dorje's teachings, I have chosen a second method to record his teachings. I have chosen to enfold his teachings into the structure of what is called in Buddhism "The Six Perfections".[8] This is a purely subjective choice; however, it does provide some context. It is said that all the advice that the Buddha gave could be summed up in the six perfections. These six perfections are:

---

[8] *These are also referred to as "The Six Paramitas."*

1. Generosity
2. Virtue (Ethical Discipline)
3. Patience
4. Diligence (Enthusiastic Effort)
5. Contemplation
6. Wisdom

The ability to accomplish these perfections depends on an uninterrupted series of good rebirths in which one enjoys positive conditions for continued spiritual practice such as plentiful resources, a strong body and mind, and supportive fellow practitioners. The practice of the six perfections ensures that we will gain favorable conditions for effective practice. For example, *generosity* leads to the enjoyment of ample resources. Generosity, however, cannot protect us from a bad rebirth in which it is impossible to make good use of these resources. How often do we hear of individuals inheriting great wealth only to squander these gifts through careless spending and indulgent lifestyles? Restraint from such actions requires *virtue or ethical discipline*, thus insuring a favorable rebirth. In addition, the practice of *patience* brings supportive friends and companions into our life. Along with the aspiration of living a virtuous life, the help of friends and spiritual practitioners supports us through the inevitable challenges that visit our lives.

Diligence, or *enthusiastic effort*, endows us with the ability to complete what we undertake. This effort keeps us moving in the right direction to attain enlightened body, speech and mind. However, even if we have conducive circumstances, our actions will not be effective as long as the mind is scattered and distracted. Thus, we must practice *contemplation* or *concentration* to create positive energy and make our mind invulnerable to distraction. Additionally, unless we also possess *wisdom* to discriminate between what needs to be cultivated and what must be discarded, we will consume the stock of positive energy created by wholesome actions. By cultivating wisdom, we are able to ensure that we never lack creative and new positive energy. Finally, we must be aware that our wish to possess these qualities of perfection is first and foremost for the benefit of others. By fulfilling the needs of others through practicing the six perfections, everything we wish for ourselves will be accomplished.

So, with this structure in mind, I will try to convey some of Lama Dorje's teachings on these subjects. But as you read these teachings, bear in mind one fundamental factor: Lama Dorje has many years of experience working with Western students. He has great understanding of the Western mind and how it works. He knows we want instant gratification. He knows we are impatient for results. He knows we would rather talk than act. He knows we value speed above depth of accomplishment. He knows our attention span can at times be minuscule. As a result, Lama's teachings are succinct and direct. They are not filled with lengthy explanations, academic references or flowery speech. They just simply tell it like it is! Be prepared!

GENEROSITY

While we often think of generosity in the context of giving material things such as money, food or clothing, the true concept of generosity is more far-reaching. In the Buddhist tradition, generosity is often defined as *"a virtuous mental decision to give, or a physical or verbal act of giving that is motivated by a virtuous mind."* In addition to the giving of tangible items, it indicates as well intangible things like time, protection, emotional support and the like. Generosity is the first of the six perfections. Many Buddhist texts describe generosity as *"the willingness to give"* whether it is one's body, one's possessions or one's energy.

Lama Dorje says:

It is sometimes hard to talk about generosity to Western people because you may think I am asking for money. I am not asking for money. Generosity is more than money. Generosity means more than the giving of material things. For example, you may see a rich man walking down the road. Maybe he trips and falls down. Although he is rich, he may be old or crippled. He may be so old and crippled that when he falls down, he cannot get up. All his money cannot pick him up. But a young boy who has no money comes walking down the road and sees the rich man has fallen. The young boy stops and picks up the old and crippled man. Now the young boy has no money to give. He has no possessions to share. But what he does have is a generous mind ... a virtuous mind ... and with his generous mind, he gives help to the old man who has fallen. You should think about generosity in this way.

Lama also says:

Generosity also helps us overcome attachment. We get attached to many things ... books ... clothes ... even thoughts and ideas. If you listen when people talk, they say "My book ... my coat ... My ideas. But these things are impermanent. If we get attached to them, they will only bring us suffering. When we die, we cannot take our books. When we die, we must leave our beautiful clothes behind. When we die, our thoughts and

53

our ideas disappear. So, if we are generous, we break some of the clinging to things. We break some of the attachment.

And when you give, you should not give thinking you will get something in return. If you give something to your boss, you may think, "Oh, now, my boss will like me and he will give me a raise." No, this is not giving with generosity. This is more like a business deal. You give something and get something in return. This is not true giving. This is not true generosity. Give freely, without expectation.

I have witnessed Lama's generosity time and time again. For many many years, he refused a salary from the Center. Even when people gave him donations directly, he refused to use that money on himself. He unfailingly saved this money for Dharma use, sometimes contributing it to do needed repairs to the stupa. Often he used it to help pay for the construction of stupas or buildings to house the Kangyur texts and a limitless number of uses to support and further the Dharma.

Lama is equally generous with his time. He never gives up on anyone. He always gives them advice, instructions and teachings regardless of how many times he has shared his knowledge and wisdom with them in the past. I know this for a fact for I was one of his students who often had to have lessons repeated and repeated before I finally understood.

And he is equally generous with his actions. Over the years, I watched Lama fully and physically engage in working harder than any paid employee to accomplish and complete Dharma projects. At the KSK Center, I have seen him work on endless projects to improve the facilities. Some of these projects were glamorous and dramatic like white-washing the stupa and some were totally utilitarian and nasty like clearing out sewage from a malfunctioning septic tank. At the Taos Center he worked diligently side by side with Norbert, Gal and the KDC sangha to complete the building of a stupa, a meditation building, a retreat house and a building to house the Kangyur texts. All of these structures were built in an area where little more than chamisa, sagebrush and small pinon trees graced the landscape. There was no electricity and no water on this site. But still he worked hauling water, clearing brush, and digging in the hard desert dirt from which adobe bricks are made. There was no job that Lama asked the workers to do that he himself did not perform.

I watched his generosity when we drove three hours every Saturday from Santa Fe up to Questa and then three hours back to work on the Kagyu Mila Guru stupa there. When he arrived, he did not find a comfortable chair and watch while his students worked. No, he grabbed a hoe and mixed concrete in a wheelbarrow to haul up to the workers putting concrete block in place. He led by example. He did not ask his students to do any work that he himself had not done.

Lama's generosity is also a study in humility. He could easily and understandably have set himself apart from his students, serving as a supervisor rather than a worker, but he did not. Remember, in so many ways Lama is not an ordinary person. He is an extraordinary being. He is someone who has devoted his entire adult life to the work of helping all beings, someone who has spent 3 years, 3 months and 3 days in meditative retreat to gain insight and understanding into profound Buddhist teachings. He is someone who has taken 253 monastic vows, pledging his life and his sanctity to the good of the world, foregoing earthly pleasures and rewards. He is someone who clearly knows more, much more than his students about a spiritual life. But he did not use any of this to set himself apart. In the true manifestation of Guru Milarepa, one of Tibet's greatest yogis, he worked at the lowliest of jobs to yield the highest of benefits.

One of Lama's students recounts some examples of Lama's generous spirit in the following stories:

> One day when we had just started building the Kagyu Mila Guru stupa, my husband Steve jokingly told Lama Dorje that since this was now a construction site, we needed donuts. Steve had in mind one of those small boxes of donuts from local grocery stores. But not so with Lama. Ever after on that project, large boxes of Dunkin Donuts arrived with Lama, bringing considerable cheer to those who had already begun shoveling and dragging around hoses and tools by the time Lama arrived.

And then:

> Not long after that, an incident occurred involving some children. These children were not the children of those working on the stupa nor did

they live in the neighborhood. These visitors didn't come with the intention of working on the stupa as the children whose parents were working on the stupa often did. The main goal of these kids, I believe, was to convince the working kids to come and play with them. Nobody seemed to mind that much however, these kids saw the donuts and descended on them. Several adults tried to shoo them away so they wouldn't eat so many, but Lama stopped this and said these kids were hungry and we should let them eat. These kids came around several times after that and yes, they did eat quite a few donuts.

What changed for me that day was my view of these particular kids. I had, perhaps, projected my own three-square-meals-a-day mentality onto their family. It was true, as I later found out, that these kids always had a big appetite. That day though, was when I learned that just because these kids were as tall as I was, this did not necessarily mean that they had enough food. It does not matter if they can reach the top shelf of a refrigerator or cabinet. It does not matter if they live in an area where food is not only commonly available, but available in abundance. Lama Dorje just knew they were hungry and that was enough. I, on the other hand, was blinded to that by some illusion I had cultivated or that had been cultivated in my family and the times in which I grew up. I looked at their hefty eating of the donuts and judged their motivation. All Lama saw was their hunger. And his actions purged me of my assumptions right on the spot!. Maybe Lama just grew up in a country where he recognized the behavior of hungry kids or maybe ... and most likely ... Lama just knew more than I did. He just has so much more awareness.

- Anna R.

Not only does Lama encourage generosity towards people, but all other creatures as well. A student of Lama's relates a teaching which Lama gave him:

I teach my students to always be kind and care for animals. Students at my center in Santa Fe are quite sensitive to the needs of animals and buy food for the birds, food for the stray cats, and carrots and hay for the bunnies. These animals get pleasure from these gifts. The students feel their hearts soften as they feed the animals, and all of this makes me endlessly happy.

Helping animals is a selfless action. I call on you to provide similar kindness to the animals in your yard and world. It is important to pay attention to these kinds of animals not only by praying for them but for caring for them as well. These animals have no owners. These animals have no food. These animals have no home. We can provide help. The birds in the winter cannot find insects to eat. We can feed them. In the spring and summer they have new baby birds. They cannot find enough food for their babies. We must feed them even more so that they can feed their babies. We must help them, or the baby birds will die. We can make bird houses and special places for them to nest. In the winter, the bunnies have nothing to eat as the snow and cold kill all the plants. We must care for them and feed them. In the summer we worry that the bunnies will eat our gardens. Do not worry. We can let them have it and even give them a special treat of carrots. This is all an opportunity for generosity. We must not be stingy. Stinginess is no good. Instead of helping animals, we fight them and complain about them. This is not right. They need our generosity. Let the gophers have your plants. Let the squirrels eat your flower buds. Rejoice that you helped a living being! We can make a place in our yard for compost for the ants and the earthworms.

If you care for these beings, it will come back to you. This type of generosity accumulates lots of positive karma. Many people want to be successful with their business. Many people want to be successful with their wife or husband. Many people want to have health and good luck. If one notices all of the suffering of animals and tries to alleviate it, then all successes will be fulfilled.

- *Aaron G.*

One of the most personal stories Lama has shared is about his pet dog named Rowdy. Rowdy was a medium-sized dog of mixed breeds. He was not especially cuddly nor did he tolerate strangers very well, if at all. But he was deeply devoted to Lama Dorje. He followed him everywhere, including into the stupa for meditation. Lama taught Rowdy to do prostrations and when he came into the stupa, he would prostrate three times before the statue of Lord Buddha. Then, he would go over and sit or lie down next to Lama. He also had another distinguishable quality and I tell it with all due respect: Rowdy often graced the interior of the stupa and those of us seated for meditation, with a silent, but deadly, fart!

Lama speaks tenderly of Rowdy even to this day:

Many people around the world care for animals by having a pet. This is a good way to help a being by giving it a home and giving it food, companionship, love and affection. I once had a pet named Rowdy. He was very special to me and a very good dog despite his moments of "rowdiness." He would follow me from room to room. Wherever I went, he wanted to be standing by my side. We had lots of wonderful years together. Eventually, he passed away and I was very sad. I experienced so much suffering from having to let go of him. I decided that I could no longer have a pet because it was too much suffering to have to say good-by and bury them. I still miss Rowdy, but this experience opened my heart further to the many other animals all around the center.

Despite deciding not to have another pet, many animals have come to my house and I have cared for them. I have paid attention to them and their habits with some degree of curiosity in an effort to see what they need. At one point, I noticed that the smaller birds were being eaten by predators like hawks and cats. I built a bird sanctuary by making a small platform, 5 feet long and 5 feet wide inside a fenced in area with chicken wire that I filled with lots and lots of tree branches. When a hawk would come, the small birds could escape by tunneling in to the center of the refuge into small spaces between the branches. The hawks could not catch them there. Caring for these birds had its own rewards of listening to the songs of hundreds of birds all day long. I find it incredibly peaceful to watch and listen to bird songs. Other people would come to my house and hear the birds, delighting in their songs too. Caring for these birds brought joy to me, joy to the birds and joy to everyone who saw it and heard them sing. That is the power of generosity. Generosity to animals brings happiness, pleasure and inspiration.

Those of us who attended meditation practice regularly at the KSK stupa saw Lama's kindness to animals. We also saw his care and protection for his birds. And we remember well his treatment of a hawk that Lama caught nose-diving after the little birds. As students have described it:

Lama always had an affinity for birds and he was able to catch them in his hands. He made sure there was always food available for them. Next to his house, there was a large bush-like structure that Lama had built as a place for the small birds to gather. One day he said to me, "I have a bird in federal prison." He brought out a raptor that he had wrapped in a towel and he proceeded very gently, placing small pieces of menudo [tripe] in its mouth, stroking its throat so it would swallow. The hawk had been killing the little birds so Lama captured it and caged it for three days to save some little birds lives.

-Rachel S.

I once tried to give Lama Dorje a beautiful woolen tsen ... the shawl-like cloth that Buddhist monks wear. The tsen had been given to me by the Khenpo at KTD. I was shocked to see the tsen of Lama Dorje's that was so threadbare and virtually useless against the cold. His tsen was badly moth-eaten. Lama refused to accept my gift. In an act of true humility, he expressed concern for the moths and for me ... putting his own needs last.

-Paul S.

As you can see, Lama Dorje did not just talk about generosity, he demonstrated it in his every action. No person was too small or no situation too insignificant to escape his tireless acts of generosity. What a living example and a living teaching he gives.

ETHICAL DISCIPLINE

Ethics and vows are of great importance in all traditions of Buddhism. As a fully ordained Tibetan Buddhist monk, Lama Dorje has taken 253 vows.[9] Of the vows that Lama Dorje has taken, five of them are vows which anyone wishing to follow the Tibetan Buddhist path may take. These vows are agreeing to avoid:

1. Killing
2. Stealing
3. Sexual Misconduct
4. Lying
5. Intoxicants

I can truly say that in the thirty-plus years that I have known Lama Dorje, I have never known him to break any of these vows. I have never seen him kill anything. On the contrary, I have seen him pick up birds lying on the ground that were seemingly dead, hold them in his hands, recite prayers over them, blow his breath into their faces and watch them come alive.

I have never known him to steal anything or even innocently assume that something was his when it was not. What I have seen him do many times too numerous to count, is give away things to others that were given to him. And as one who helped him manage his personal finances for many years, almost every single donation he received went back into dharmic activity. He didn't buy clothes with the money. He wore only the clothes that were given to him. He didn't send money home to his family. He used it to further dharmic activity in this country. And he would give money to beggars. For many

---

[9] *By way of background, these vows, called vinaya, are set forth in an ancient text called, in translation, the Individual Liberation Sutras. These vows were brought to Tibet by the Indian Abbot Shantarakshita in the 8th century. At the request of the Tibetans, Shantarakshita founded the first monastic community by first ordaining seven young and promising Tibetans. Ever since this monastic tradition was established in Tibet, it has continued unbroken despite great difficulties in times when Buddhist monasteries and Buddhists in general were subject to persecution.*

years we traveled to Lama's center in Taos or up to Questa to work on the stupa there. We left Santa Fe early in the morning. We often stopped at Dunkin Donuts to get a cup of coffee to keep us happy on our trips north. Numerous times there would be men hanging outside of the doughnut and coffee shop whose activities the night before had obviously included the consumption of generous amounts of alcohol. Lama would often hand us a few small bills to give to these struggling and unfortunate souls.

Likewise, I have never known Lama Dorje to engage in anything even close to sexual misconduct. He works with female students equally as open and giving as he does with male students. He gives advice and teachings to both men and women and yet never does he come close to crossing any lines of intimacy. He never comes close to creating discomfort among his female students.

Lama Dorje also does not lie. He answers questions truthfully and completely. And yes, there are times when he must deliver answers and advice that are not easy. Sometimes he has to say no. But he is so amazingly skillful at giving hard answers or advice that even bad news seems wrapped in great kindness.

Lama talks often about the importance of maintaining vows you have taken. To illustrate the necessity of keeping vows, he tells a story that is told and retold in many different ways in the Buddhist tradition. He sometimes changes various details of the story, but the message is a variation of the basic theme. Here is one version of the story:

> A young monk was traveling alone through the countryside. It was the custom of the people in the country to offer traveling monks food and temporary shelter because supporting those who were devoting their lives to the Dharma was a virtuous action. Late one afternoon, the young monk approached a small village. An attractive young woman emerged from one of the tents and invited the young monk to spend the night. Having only very recently taken the vow of celibacy, it was very present in his mind. He declined her offer and replied that he still had time to walk further that day.
>
> The young woman said "Well at least stop and have something to eat before you continue on your way". The monk was actually quite hungry, and he could smell the delicious aroma coming from the food that

was being cooked. However, he knew that unless the meat used for the stew had arisen from the natural death of an animal, eating the meat would mean that he had participated in the killing of the animal. And, to avoid killing, of course, was one of the vows he had just taken. So, he declined the food.

The woman said, "Well at least stop long enough to have a drink of chang." Chang is Tibetan beer made from barley. The young monk had, of course, taken a vow to abandon intoxicants, just as he had vowed not to kill or to engage in sexual activity. Having already turned down the kind girl's first two invitations, and not wishing to cause offense, he decided to accept a small cup of chang. After taking a few sips of chang, the monk felt very relaxed. He felt quite comfortable with the woman. In fact, he felt there was a real connection between them. After a few more sips of chang, he decided to have some of the stew she offered because in truth he was quite hungry. And after eating, he felt much too tired to walk any further, so he succumbed to spending the night with the woman.

Lama uses this story not only to illustrate the importance of keeping vows but also to show how relaxing one vow often leads to a relaxation of all the vows.

But Lama Dorje can also be a bit of a trickster. He had many times given Virginia, Ted (another KSK practitioner) and I instructions about the danger of taking vows that we could not keep. He said it was better not to take the vow in the first place than to take the vow and not keep it. During that time, a visiting Lama was coming to KSK to teach. One of the teachings he was giving was about the Bodhisattva Vow. *Bodhisattva* is a Sanskrit word which is the name given to anyone who, motivated by great compassion, wishes to attain enlightenment for the benefit of all living beings. Many Buddhist texts and writings discuss the Boddhisattva Vow, both the benefit of taking the vow but also the downfalls if you take it and do not keep it.

Before this visiting Lama arrived, Virginia, Ted and I had many discussions with Lama Dorje about taking this vow. We asked Lama if we should take it. Lama shook his head and said somewhat doubtfully, *"Oh, you think you can keep this vow? You take this vow and no keep it, then that be very bad."* His advice was not very encouraging. We discussed this among ourselves and concluded that while we looked forward to hearing the teachings about the Bodhisattva Vow, we were not yet ready to take it.

The day arrived when the visiting Lama gave the Bodhisattva Vow teachings. After concluding his teachings, he prepared to administer the Vow to all who wished to take it. At that teaching Virginia, Ted and I happened to be sitting near Lama Dorje. As people in the audience came forward to sit closer to the visiting Lama to receive the Vow, I felt quite relaxed and relieved that we had decided we were not yet ready to take this Vow. Suddenly, Lama Dorje looked at us and said, *"Go. Now you go."* We looked at each other with great confusion. Lama looked at us quite sternly and again said, *"Now you go. Now you take the Vow."* So up we went. I felt moments of panic. Here I was taking a Vow, a most sacred Buddhist vow, that I was not at all certain I could keep. But following Lama's instructions, we took the Bodhisattva Vow. After the ceremony was over, I felt a great wave of apprehension. I knew the strength of my commitment to the Buddhist path. I understood the concept of living my life compassionately to try to relieve the suffering of others. But what I did not know was if I had the ability to keep this most sacred of Buddhist vows. Days later, in discussions with him, Lama Dorje relieved our anxious minds by telling us that we could take the vow as an aspirational vow. A vow that we would continue to work to achieve.

And even though this was a stern instruction from Lama Dorje, it was still Lama Dorje as a trickster. It was Lama "playing" with the minds of his student. In this way, his actions sometimes reminded me of the great yogi Tilopa whose "unusual" instructions to his student Naropa sometimes seemed to border on the absurd. Fortunately, Lama Dorje never asked us to physically jump off a building to prove our faith in the teacher! But it was as a trickster that you had the experience of Lama Dorje's humor. As one student recalls:

> *Lama Dorje knows English very well. He knows exactly what he is saying. But then sometimes when he talks, he talks in a way that you might think he doesn't really understand English. But if you know him a bit .... If you have been around him and worked with him, you know exactly what he is saying. And sometimes he says things as if it's humorous ... as if it's a joke. So you laugh along with Lama and the other folks around but then suddenly you get it! And you say "What the heck was that?" And Lama may still be smiling, but you have just received an important teaching ... sometimes a special message just for you ... even though others around you are laughing.*
>
> - *David B.*

Talking about Ethical Discipline is not easy because talking about Discipline is not easy. None of us get excited about rules. We want to live "free and easy," making rules up as we go along. But rules in spiritual practice are somewhat like learning the multiplication tables. You cannot really get the results you want if you don't know the table. After all, we soon run out of fingers to count on when we want to know the result of 5 x 5! Likewise, it is much harder to get the fruit of our practice if we do not know the rules.

Often, we think of rules as limitations ... a long and boring list of *"Do's"* and *"Do Not Do's"*. But it is sometimes helpful to think of rules in a broader context. Rules can also be great facilitators. Suppose you are making a journey and you are looking at a map to try and figure out the route to your destination. There will be many roads shown on the map. In selecting your route, you remember the adage that a straight line is the shortest distance between two points. So, you look for the most direct route. But the shortest, straight-line route may have limitations of its own. For instance, if you were traveling from north of a major city like Los Angeles, you would see major roadways that go relatively straight through that city. But what might not be apparent is that while the straight road may be fairly easy to locate on a map, there are other factors that might discourage you from taking the straight-line route. In the case of Los Angeles, one of the major considerations in taking straight-line roads is the traffic. No matter how straight the road, no matter how wide the road, when you are travelling on these roads through LA, the major impediment has little to do with the straightness of the road. Instead, in each and every lane you will be confronted with back-to-back vehicles moving at turtle-like speeds. Some roads may be wider and faster to travel on. Other roads may be small and winding. So "rules" can be helpful. Rules can facilitate your travel. Rules like "don't go through LA during commute traffic" or "Leave early in the morning if you want to make it through town with less traffic" make your journey easier. Knowing the rules in addition to the route will facilitate your travel and make your progress smoother.

So how can rules and ethical discipline facilitate our spiritual journey? Buddhism places great emphasis on restraint from harm and the creation of virtue. Ethical discipline teaches us how to follow the "rules of the road." And as any student of Lama Dorje knows or will soon learn, Lama is very clear and quite strict about following the rules. Lama Dorje is one of the kindest people I have ever known. He delivers his teachings and instructions clearly and compassionately. But when there are transgressions, he is not timid about pointing those out. I remember vividly one of those instances that occurred while we were building the Kagyu Mila Guru stupa in Questa. We were nearing the point where we needed to place a thousand tsa-tsa near the crown of the stupa. "Tsa-tsa" are small replicas of a stupa. They are about 6 inches high, made of clay or plaster with carvings on the outside, and painted gold with red on the base. Prayers are made and written on small lengths of paper that are rolled up carefully and inserted inside each tsa-tsa. Making these tsa-tsa is a time-consuming process. Lama Dorje had been making these tsa-tsa in the lean-to shed on the back side of the hut where he lived at the KSK Center. I was concerned about getting the tsa-tsa completed in time and decided I would take a day off from work and go out to the Center and help make the tsa-tsa. Here is what happened:

> *I arrived early in the morning and knocked on Lama's door to tell him that I had come to make tsa-tsa. He came to the door and immediately asked me what I was doing there. I told him I had come to help make tsa-tsa. He said, "Why aren't you at work?" I replied that I had taken the day off from work to come and help make tsa-tsa. The look on his face and the tone of his voice can best be described as "fierce." He said, "Why you do that?" Recognizing that he was far from happy about my presence there, I explained that I was allowed to take a certain number of days off from work and that is what I was doing. He was unconvinced. With the sternest of looks, he said, "You no do that. But now that you are here, you must work." He led me around to the lean-to where he had a number of tsa-tsa made. The next step in their finishing was to write the prayers, roll them into a small circle and insert them into the tsa-tsa. He told me what to do and cautioned me very sternly to do them exactly right. He said, "If you make mistake, it be bad karma for you and for me, so you no make mistake." There was nothing soft or gentle in his delivery of this warning.*

Let me hasten to add that this was not Lama Dorje's normal behavior. He always treated people doing work around the stupa or the Center with the greatest of kindness and care, usually offering them tea and maybe a cookie before beginning their work. This time no such items were offered to me. Lama showed me what to do and left me there to do it! I worked for four hours without taking a break or seeing Lama. He came once to check on what I was doing and his only comment was to once again admonish me not to make any mistakes as it would be bad karma. Trust me, I got the message. I got the teaching. The rules were clear. I would not be taking time off from work to make tsa-tsa ever again!

Lama has always spoken strongly about the importance of discipline and right action. I think it is fair to say that most of us enjoy being acknowledged for the "good" things that we do. Conversely, we generally do not like to hear about the things we have done wrong. Take for example, the experience just described about taking time off from work to make tsa-tsa. Quite frankly, I expected to be positively acknowledged, maybe even thanked kindly! On the contrary, I was chastised strongly by Lama for my efforts. Did that make me happy? No, it did not. Being on the receiving end of Lama's apparent anger was not fun!! But in looking back at this issue, I realize that Lama was not angry at me, _per se_, but he was angry because he thought my action would create bad karma. And as my spiritual guide, protecting me from accruing bad karma is high on the list of Lama's responsibilities.

Lama discusses his own experiences with being on the receiving end of someone's apparent anger. He talks about his very early times with Sarah Harding. Remember that Sarah is herself a Tibetan Buddhist Lama having been one of the first western women to complete a three-year retreat. Furthermore, she was directed by Kalu Rinpoche to assist and help Lama as he acclimated to being in the Western world. Here is what Lama says:

> We must think carefully about people's actions toward us. Sometimes bad people seem good and sometimes good people seem bad. Sometimes people understand us and then sometimes they no understand. Sometimes people like you and sometimes people no like you. And when they no like you, you think , "Oh, he be mean person." Or, "Oh, he be angry person. He only want to embarrass me." But you must think about that. Sometimes their anger wakes us up! Sometimes, it makes us say we no want to stay that way.
>
> But then sometimes people say we are special. And we think, "Oh what nice person they are to say that. Oh, they think I am special." And then pretty soon you start to think that you are special. You start to be

proud. And your ego is proud. But if you think you are so good and so special, you never grow. If someone fusses at you, it makes you stop and think, "Oh. What am I doing wrong?" And then you think about that and you grow.

Example, when I first come here, Sarah Harding looks sometimes like my enemy. She shout bad things at me and she get angry at me. And I think, oh she no like me. She no understand. But now I know that she shouted these bad things at me to teach me... she wanted me to learn ... like a mother teaching her child. One time she and me were driving to Taos and we were drinking a bottle of coke. When I finished my bottle, I rolled down the window in the car and threw the bottle out alongside the road. Sarah got very angry at me and she shout at me. She say, "You no do that!" You no throw out trash on the road." I say, "Well I am India kind. I no understand." And she got even angrier and she say "Well you live here and you must live like people here live. You no throw trash out the window." She drove the car back and we picked up the bottle. I felt very bad because I think she so angry with me. I think she no like me. But no. She is teaching me. She is like a mother teaching her child. If the mother no teach then the child will do bad things. Now I am not a child. I am a big man but my understanding was like a child and she teach me. Like a mother teaches a child.

One other time I go over to her house. I knock on the door but she no answer. I think maybe she no hear me and I walk into her house. But she be in bathroom, and she get very angry with me. She tell me you no come into my house when I am in the bathroom. So that she also teach me. In my country, nothing. You come inside and they tell you I in the bathroom doing. But she teach me. Must not go into her house if she no answers the door and is in the bathroom. Same thing as when you come to see me. You announce that you are here. You say, Hi Lama. This is Alice as you come down the hall. And here if you no say it ... if you no announce yourself, people think you're sneaky. You knock so people know you are coming. This Sarah teach me like mother teach her child.

Many times I think she mean to me and she not like me and she angry with me but now I understand. I am not always good. I am not always bad. But wrongdoing must tell because that is how you grow. Before one time when I was in Los Angeles, the Karmapa and many monks came. I also was there together with them. We prepare lots of food and were sending to the Karmapa and the monks and they were eating.

And then they were resting. But I no go where they are. I was sending things but I no go. Then Sarah comes and says "What are you doing here? Why aren't you out there with the Karmapa?" Then she pulled my hand and take me over there. Otherwise, I no go. No one invited me. I am thinking they are special and I no special. I send things but I no go unless they invite. But Sarah really fussed at me. She said "Why you do that? Why you no go?" I tell her in India you no do that. The Karmapa and his people are special and you no go unless they invite you. She got very mad and she grabbed me and said, "Why are you waiting?" "You go!" And then she pushed me to go. Many times Sarah Harding did these things and I think she mad at me. But she no mad at me ... she teaching me.

Even Lama remains open to learning and growing. Although his state of being is far superior to anything or anyone I have ever met, he remains humble when others might protest. He does not hold himself apart and superior even when he could justifiably do so. He sees the lesson in every moment and in every event. And his example of letting each moment and each event teach us is extremely powerful. Asking yourself the question, *"What would Lama do?"* allows us to grow. Seeing the teaching in every moment allows us to move beyond the reaction of the ego and converts what might otherwise be a trying and difficult moment into a valuable lesson for our own evolution.

PATIENCE

Much has been said, much has been written, and much has been observed about patience. Still, patience remains elusive. I know in my own life it is a quality that I have tried to acquire over and over again with only modest results. I am a "doer." I like to make things happen and I like to make them happen *now*! Years ago, my mother gave me a beautiful piece of embroidery that she had made for me that said, *"God, grant me patience, and make it quick!!"* But practicing patience just for the sake of practicing patience in a hypothetical way doesn't necessarily translate into being patient. This is where Lama Dorje's teaching style makes a difference.

Lama Dorje does not talk about patience, or any similar virtue, in an abstract way. Lama's teachings are always grounded in practicality, not theory. Lama reminds us that we all want to be happy. We do not want to be sad. But life's challenges and life's experiences do not always bring happiness. On the contrary, life often brings pain and suffering. Lama might ask you, *"Do you want to be happy?"* You would emphatically answer "YES!" Then he would ask, *"So why are you sad?" "Why are you unhappy?"* You might recount that you got into an argument with someone, and they made you angry because they said unkind or untrue things about you. You might add, as I often did, that the person "hurt your feelings." Lama would look at you and ask, *"So what is hurt?" "Do you have two eyes? Are your eyes hurt?"* NO. *You have a nose. Is your nose hurt?"* NO. *You have two ears, are your ears hurt?"* NO. *You have two arms, are your arms hurt?"* And so forth until you agreed that your arms and legs and feet, in fact, your entire body was not hurt. Then Lama might say, *"Well, why then are you unhappy? Why are you sad? You are not hurt."*

Then pushing a little harder, you might remind Lama that this person made you angry. At this point Lama might say, *"So it is really your anger that is making you unhappy. It is your anger that is destroying your peace of mind."* Reluctantly, you might acknowledge that this was so. Then Lama might say, *"So what can you do about your anger?"* And slowly but surely, Lama would lead you around to explaining that patience was an antidote for anger. He would suggest that you look at the person who had "hurt" you and see that the problem was not the person who angered you, but your own anger itself. If you want to avoid being hurt, if you want to avoid being angry, then you must learn the antidote. You must learn patience. Now suddenly, patience is no longer just an abstract thought. It has genuine purpose in your life and genuine support to fend off anger and the distress that anger brings.

I once discussed with Lama a situation with an individual who had said unkind things about me in several public forums. The things the person said were untrue. I felt my anger was justified. After a discussion similar to the one mentioned above, Lama brought the discussion back to learning patience. And he gave me a tool that was extremely helpful. He said:

> *"Think of this person as having a serious illness. If, for example, this person had a physical problem with his mouth. Maybe his mouth was injured in an accident leaving him facially deformed and unable to speak." Lama said, "You would feel sad for this person. You would feel sorry for his physical deformity. You would feel compassion for the challenges those things had brought to his life." I acknowledged that I would. Then Lama said, "Well, think of this individual as having a mental sickness. Think of his mind as being deformed. Think of his mental sickness as making him unable to recognize the truth or to speak the truth." Suddenly, I saw my situation from an entirely different viewpoint. Suddenly, I genuinely felt compassion for someone who was unable to speak the truth. My anger was gone and along with it, my unhappiness. Lama said, "Be patient with these types of people. Do not be angry but practice patience."*

Suddenly, patience was no longer an unattainable virtue to be cultivated in the abstract. It was an authentic and genuine cure for my unhappiness.

Another student of Lama Dorje's shared a similar lesson in patience. He recounts his experiences dealing with an unkind and somewhat dishonest co-worker.

> *When I was working in restaurants, one night I worked harder than I ever had before. At the end of the night when I was cashing out, the manager decided that he was keeping half my tips because he claimed he had helped me out so much! I was furious and I let him know it. The next day I visited Lama Dorje at my usual time. He asked, "How doing?" Like*

72

a can of soda pop just shaken, my anger about what had happened raged to the top. I told Lama the story and ended saying fervently, "He stole my money!" Lama listened very quietly without any apparent emotion. He looked at me and said very clearly and very simply, "I know it's hard, but don't fight. Let him have the money. No big deal. Money come and money go." I was still upset and said to Lama, "But that's not fair to me! That is just letting him steal from me!" Lama repeated, "Don't fight. Give him the money. Generosity good. Maybe he need the money. He have it. No problem."

As hard as it was to follow Lama's advice, I did. The next night we worked together, I let my competitor have the tip money from all the tables. As I was leaving, my competitor offered me a table to wait on. Swallowing my pride, I said, "That's OK. You take it. I hope you make lots of money." At my next shift with this competitor, he acted completely different towards me. He helped me with my work and at the end of the night, he gave me all of my tips.

The next day, I told Lama this story. He said, "Be careful. Do not get attached to things. Do not get attached to money. When you get attached, arguments come. Always practice kindness, then money always come. You always searching for money. What for? Fifty dollars be good. Twenty dollars, not bad. You are a lucky man. Everything you have. Some people have no money. Some people have nothing. You rich. Appreciate everything or everything gone." I have experienced many amazing things during my time with Lama Dorje, but my most powerful experiences have been the results of applying his advice. His simple advice has made my life feel like paradise.

- *Aaron G.*

This advice from Lama Dorje combines many qualities. At its simplest, it is a lesson about generosity, but perhaps more importantly, it is a lesson about patience ... patience with other people and patience with their weaknesses and limitations. It is one thing to hear advice. It is another thing to understand the advice. But it is still a more challenging thing to be able to apply this advice in our lives. It takes facing our ego straight on. It takes tamping down our anger about being "wronged." And then it takes great patience to let go and seemingly give the "victory" to others.

As many of Lama's students can attest, Lama is an enormously patient person. When you talk with him, he listens and he listens carefully. He hears what your concerns and questions are, but perhaps more importantly, he hears your unspoken cares and concerns. Many times I have spoken with Lama about a concern I had and he listens yet appears sometimes to treat it lightly. Then, even before I realize it, Lama will suddenly start talking about something completely different. While I wonder why he is doing this, I realize moments, sometimes hours or days later that he was actually addressing an issue that I had been unable to bring up in our discussion. For example, I remember once discussing with Lama some concerns about a particular practice I was learning. I thought he answered my concern rather casually but then he started talking about skillfulness in our interactions with people. More specifically, he was talking about the care we must use when delivering "bad news" to people.

At the time, this discussion, while interesting, seemed completely unrelated to my question about my meditation practice, a question he had treated rather lightly. It was only after I left Lama Dorje and was driving home that I realized that Lama had spoken to the one great concern that I had not articulated about needing to "fire" one of my employees. Firing someone is never easy and was really weighing on my mind. I had not mentioned this concern to Lama Dorje, but I realized that his discussion about "skillfulness in delivering bad news," was a complete and true answer to my unspoken concern about this employee. It taught me that when seeking advice from Lama, one had to always be aware that your agenda and Lama's agenda might be different, and quite wonderfully so!

Lama's patience was often most wonderfully evident during meditation practice itself. In the Stupa, after we had completed whatever particular practice we were doing, Lama often gave a "teaching." He also would patiently answer any questions that those present might have. The range of those questions was remarkable going all the way from *"What should I say to my dying grandmother?"* to *"What should I feed my cat?"* But Lama answered them all, sometimes in a manner that revealed his wonderful sense of humor!

And for those who claimed, *"Lama never gives teachings,"* I can only say that perhaps they had never attended a meditation practice with Lama Dorje, because after practice, Lama gave some profound teachings. For those who heard them, these teachings were like "icing on the cake!" One of Lama's students recalls the following:

I remember Lama talking after Chenrezig practice on Sunday nights. This was always really fun. One evening he described all the protective deities on the wall of the stupa opposite the shrine. He explained all of them in detail and it was a really perfect time. In fact, it was magical! No matter what was going on in the outside world or even in our personal world, being at KSK doing this practice with Lama and listening to his explanations felt like being in the pure land. Lama really built something special ... in the stupa and in our minds.

- Will F.

We often speak of patience as a virtue ... and it is. It is a virtue worth acquiring. But patience is not something one can instantly obtain. We cannot walk into our local grocery store and pluck a can of patience off the shelf. Patience is a skill, a skill we must work to possess. And like most skills we acquire, patience takes time and practice. It also requires us to remain conscious, conscious of our actions as well as conscious of the actions of others. Lama Dorje's lessons in patience were sometimes most profound in just observing how he handled situations. Many times students ask the same questions over and over. Rather than confront them with the repetitious nature of their question, he patiently and sincerely answers them. He answers these same questions without judgment and without embarrassing the questioners by reminding them that they have asked this same question many times before. Patterning our practice of patience after skilled and enlightened teachers like Lama Dorje propels us a long way on the road to developing the virtue we know as patience.

DILIGENCE – ENTHUSIASTIC EFFORT

There is an old expression which says, *"Anything worth doing is worth doing well."* I think this applies to the perfection known as diligence or enthusiastic effort. The concept of diligence itself carries a kind of heavy feeling, a bit of the old *"keep your nose to the grindstone"* flavor. I prefer the term "enthusiastic effort." People often talk in these contemporary times of "following your passion." Enthusiastic effort has that same essence, not just doing something because you are supposed to do it but doing something because it brings you joy. It expresses your passion.

Think back in your life to something that you really enjoyed doing. Maybe it was flying a kite, maybe it was making bread, maybe it was painting a mural on a classroom wall. The object of your effort was not really as important as the feelings you had about doing the thing. Capture that feeling in your mind and think about it in the context of your Buddhist practice. And what is your Buddhist practice? Is it sitting in meditation chanting from the Buddhist texts? Is it reading books about Buddhism and learning the meaning of things? Do you have to be sitting on a cushion to meditate? A wise teacher once advised, *"Make every moment a meditation. Your work is your meditation. Your family is your meditation. Your walking is your meditation."*

Lama Dorje says:

> *There are three things you need for meditation practice. In Tibetan these are called* **tam pa sum**. *These three things are:*
> 1. *Refuge*
> 2. *Prayers for the Deities*
> 3. *Dedication*
>
> *Sometimes people want to take only the big teachings, but you must first know the foundations. It is like a fruit tree; people always want the big fruit. But you cannot get the big fruit or any kind of fruit from the tree unless the tree has good roots and is in good soil and has plenty of water. The same is true of our meditation practice. We cannot expect to get the big fruit off our meditation tree unless we have first taken care of the roots and the trunk.*

Taking care of your meditation tree requires diligence and discipline. We cannot pour lots of water on the tree one day and then forget to water it entirely for the next weeks. You might manage to keep the tree alive with this flood or famine approach, but it will not thrive. It thrives from careful and consistent treatment. In much the same way, we cannot abandon our meditation for several weeks at a time and then expect twenty-four hours of straight meditation to cure our neglect.

But if we approach meditation with some enthusiasm, the responsibility of keeping our meditation tree watered, becomes far more joyful. Again, using the tree as an example, it is helpful to focus on the rewards. Suppose you love peaches, and you plant a peach tree. You put it in good soil, and you water it. You are happy to do this because you have the prospect of the reward of juicy, delicious peaches. Just thinking about those peaches makes watering your peach tree a joyful thing to do. Applying enthusiasm about the reward, makes our daily diligence far more appealing. As one teacher has said, *"Enlightenment is certainly possible for those prepared to put enthusiastic effort into the practice of Bodhisattva deeds."* Enlightenment would be an incredible fruit to pick from our meditation tree. And practicing the deeds of a Bodhisattva would provide our lives with the care and water that promise delightful rewards.

During the early years with Lama Dorje, attendance at meditation practices at KSK was modest. Often there would be only 3 or 4 practitioners at a meditation session. But the number of attendees never changed the way in which Lama Dorje conducted practice nor was it seen by Lama as a statement of success if there were lots of people attending. Practice was practice and was always the same. In so many ways those early days of practice were special. Lama has a beautiful voice and he always led the chanting. We learned to follow along in the text. We chanted in Tibetan following the texts which contained a line showing the phonetical pronunciation of the Tibetan words. Lama chanted different tunes depending on the practice. For instance, if we were doing Chenrezig practice, Lama chanted a certain tune. When we were doing Green Tara practice, Lama would chant with a different tune. These tunes were quite beautiful and made chanting in another language much easier to follow.[10]

During those early times, a photographer named Ted joined our regular little practice sessions. Ted and Virginia and I became good Dharma friends. Ted had a very analytical mind and he would often do research on various aspects of Buddhist practice. He kindly shared his findings with Virginia and me and we each helped the other learn the Buddhist practices. Lama Dorje was always our guide and he taught us many of the "rights" and "wrongs" of the various meditation practices that we did. He taught us kindly and gently, but when we made mistakes that he had previously taught us, he wasted no time in pointing out our deficiencies!! Even though at times those "pointing out" instructions hurt out egos, I came to understand what a gift these "pointing out instructions" were.

In those early days, Virginia, Ted and I were often referred to as Lama's "Three Musketeers." We were, admittedly, eager and enthusiastic to learn and I imagine that to some we seemed a bit childish and naïve in our approach. But our hearts were in the right place and even now, many years later, I cherish those times that we shared together with Lama Dorje. Lama often talked about the rewards of practice and encouraged us to persevere in our meditation. Most of us have heard stories about the almost magical things that can happen in meditation. A meditator who could sit for hours, never needing the sustenance of food or water, would suddenly see glorious colored rainbows, hear music of unworldly glory and then poof! receive instant enlightenment, suddenly changing their lives from the ordinary into the remarkable. Those stories, while fascinating to read or hear about, are, I believe, somewhat mythical. They make exciting tales to tell but are not always borne out in reality.

---

[10] *I am reminded of the time as a child when I learned a little French song that said:*
> *Sur le pont d'Avignon,*
> *L'on y danse, l'on y danse,*
> *Sur le pont d"Avignon*
> *L'on y danse tout en rond.*
I had no idea at the time what the words meant exactly and could never have recited it in English but because it had a catchy tune, I memorized and recited it in French! Chanting in Tibetan and learning the texts is somewhat like that. Understanding comes with time and practice.

Lama gave a teaching which, after some years of meditation practice, I came to regard as profound. Lama said that doing practice was like taking a tiny sesame seed between your fingers. You pick it up. You examine it. You rub it between your fingers for some time and eventually, a tiny little drop of oil comes out of the seed and drops into your little cup. Then you do this again with another sesame seed and after you rub it and rub it you again get a small drop of oil into your cup. If you keep doing this over and over again, eventually these small, tiny drops of oil will begin to fill your little cup. Then, when your cup is filled with the oil from these little sesame seeds, you can place a small thread inside it, strike a match to the thread, and the whole bowl lights up!

Lama said this was like doing meditation practice. We do practice over and over again. We sometimes think, "Oh, we do this same thing, this same practice, over and over again. I want to do something new; I want to do something different." But, Lama said, *"Practice is like the small sesame seed. We have to rub it and rub it, over and over again, and if we are lucky, we may get a tiny, small drop of oil, a tiny, small drop of understanding."*

I have experienced the truth of this teaching. I have done Chenrezig practice many times. No matter how many times I do this practice, no matter how many times I think I understand this practice, something new always comes through. Many, many times I have recited the refuge prayer. And yet just one morning recently, I understood something new about the wisdom of this prayer. In practice, we talk about how we want to do whatever we do to help bring all sentient beings to enlightenment. Many, many times as I have said this prayer, I have also wondered, "How can I, such a small and unlearned person, possibly ever have the skill and wisdom to bring any sentient being to enlightenment?" The answer, of course, is that by myself, this would be an extremely difficult task. And this is why we do the refuge prayer. In that prayer, we enlist the wisdom and support of the Buddhas, the Lamas, the Dharma and the Sangha. With the wisdom and blessings of these enlightened beings, anything is possible.

Lama Dorje also reminds us:

> *Too much sitting is not good for beginning people. Sit only for 10-15 minutes. And prayer is very important ... whatever your tradition. The Christians have CHRIST. The Buddhists have BUDDHA. Listening is also very important. Listen and then think about what you have heard. Ask yourself, "Is this person telling the truth?" If we think so, then we may have a karmic connection with this person. And too much talking is not good. It sometimes brings hurt to people. But when we get hurt, we should remember how this feels. Then, we will not want to do this to other people. The remembrance of hurt provides great motivation.*

I clearly remember the advice that Lama Dorje gave me once when I did a solitary, three-day meditation retreat. I was in a nice comfortable cabin in a safe environment. Yet, while I was there, I kept feeling afraid. This feeling of fear made it difficult to even sleep at night. I was concerned that perhaps I had done something wrong that brought this "scary" feeling. When I returned from my retreat, I talked to Lama Dorje about my experience. I asked him what I had done to bring on those feelings of fear. Lama's answer surprised me and was not an answer I anticipated. He said that feeling afraid was a good thing because it kept me alert during my entire meditation retreat! He said my fear was a friend.

CONTEMPLATION

While enthusiastic effort keeps us moving in the right direction, our actions will not be effective if our mind is distracted and confused. Our diligence in practice needs to be followed by contemplation or concentration to keep our mind steady and clear. Endless volumes have been written about meditation and meditation practice. In this so-called information age, we suffer not from a lack of information but from "information overload." This can happen with meditation practice as well. Understanding the Western mind as he does, Lama Dorje has given many teachings about meditation and focus. Lama says:

Many teachers come here to our KSK Center and teach many different practices and give many different empowerments and initiations. People take many of these initiations and make vows concerning these practices. You should be very careful about this because sometimes when a person makes many vows and does many practices, confusion and guilt can arise. The person may feel guilty because he does not have the time to do all the practices that he has committed to do. And this feeling of guilt interferes with his overall feelings about dharma practice. In the same way, some people will do one practice for a while and then change to another practice. Then when they need the strength that a particular deity provides, they become confused and do not know where to turn.

For example, the doors of this stupa have many different panels. Some people have as many practices as the panels on these doors. Maybe they do one practice this month ... then another practice next month ... and then another practice the next month. But in this way, they do not develop a strong connection to any one practice, and this can lead to confusion. It is very important for you to pick one practice and make a strong commitment to do this practice for a long, long time.

I will tell you a story about this. When I first came to Santa Fe, my first impressions were that it was very hot and dry here and that there were many lightning storms. I was actually quite afraid of all the lightning and how one minute the sky would be quite clear and then all of a sudden, there would be this large crack of lightning ... without much warning sometimes. Well, once when we were working here on the stupa, Chagdud Tulku Rinpoche visited. He was constructing the beautiful Buddha statue that we have here in the stupa. I told him about the lightning here. He said he was not afraid. Later, he was under the tent working on the Buddha statue. I was over in the living room at the Center fixing tea for some other Lamas who were here visiting. Suddenly, there was a great crack of lightning near the tent where Chagdud Tulku was working. He was quite alarmed by this and he came hurrying into the living room where we were having tea. After telling us what had happened, he hurried back to the tent and immediately started making a small statue of Padmasambhava. He did this while asking for protection. Chagdud Tulu knows and teaches many practices and yet when he felt concerned about the lightning, he turned to Padmasambhava, his root deity.

This is why it is important to have a strong connection with a deity so you will know where to turn when you need help and protection. If you practice to this deity one month and another deity the next month, you do not establish a strong connection with any one deity and then you will not know where to turn when you need help. You may be confused.

Contemplation is also necessary to understand and absorb what we have read and heard. We can hear the most profound teachings, we can read the most profound books, or we can be in the presence of the most profound teachers. But, in the midst of all this goodness, it will have little effect on our lives unless and until we take the time to think about what we have heard and what we have read. Lama says:

When you receive teachings, it is most important that you listen and think about what you have heard. For example, suppose you have a cup that you want to fill with wisdom. You go to hear teachings given by some wise person. But at the teachings, you have other things on your mind and you don't really hear what is being said. Sometimes you don't really listen and your mind wanders to other things. In effect, your cup is turned over. The teachings roll off your cup and no wisdom enters.

Then sometimes you hear the teachings but you don't really think about them. You hear the words but you don't really meditate about what they mean. You don't really apply them to your own life. We say you are listening with a cup full of holes. The teachings may have reached your cup, but they run out through the holes and are lost.

But when you listen carefully and then meditate about what you have heard, when your cup is right side up without holes, your cup of wisdom will gradually begin to fill up. Your cup will accumulate wisdom, So, it is most important to listen to the teachings and then think about what you have heard if you want to receive maximum benefit.

84

Contemplation or meditation has major and measurable advantages. It has very practical applications. In our world today, everyone is busy, busy, busy. We race from one activity to another, from one thought to another. Multi-tasking is a favored attribute. We say, "Look at her! She is amazing. She can do three different jobs all at once. She is a great multi-tasker." Certainly, life often demands multi-tasking: a baby is crying while a pot of chili is boiling over on the stove and then the telephone rings. We have to be very nimble to meet all these situations. But sometimes, all the demands of the various tasks we are charged with can quickly become overwhelming. As we race from one demand to the next, we give a little bit of ourselves to every single little task. We run from one expectation to the next never feeling like we have done any one thing very well. As the old adage goes, we become a "jack of all trades and a master of none." Meditation gives us a break. Meditation gives us a chance to "stop the world and let us get off." Meditation helps us to train our minds to lay down the mental noise and calmly focus. As Lama Dorje instructed, it allows us to stop and listen and fill our cup of wisdom.

Once I said to Lama Dorje, as we looked towards the canyons facing El Rito, that the masses of granite looked like three bears. Lama Dorje said, "Once you see them, you will always see them." This cryptic saying, like so many from Lama, rattled around in my mind for some time. Maybe his meaning was obvious to others, but for me it brought up a question. I often wondered about people who saw fairies, spoke to saints, or were touched by devas. I seemed to have a fascination with unseen realms. I wondered, "Was Lama referring to elemental forces inhabiting a face in a rock? What was he referring to? Once a person begins to see the world of spirit, did it become ever more visible to them?"

Years after walking down a path with a rock beside it in which anyone could easily imagine two eyes quite clearly, I finally understood what Lama meant. Once I projected an imagine of two human-looking eyes on some swirls in a rock, I would always see those swirls as eyes because I cannot see the world except through the filter of my own projections. Lama's seemingly inconsequential statement that once we see something a certain way, we will always see it that way, stayed with me. It opened some space in my mind to stop from time to time and remember that the event, the object or the world, in general, was seen through the projection of my own mind. Realizing this enabled me to sometimes change my opinion and re-examine situations outside my own, perhaps sometimes limited, projections.

-   Anna R.

Lama often asks us to contemplate the many ways in which we may help sentient beings. He sometimes asks us to contemplate how we can help animals. As he told one of his students:

Meditation is important but so is the practice of feeding beings and making sure their needs are met. Animals are very important and we must care for them. In Tibetan Buddhism cosmology, we talk about beings in the six realms: hell realms, hungry ghost realms, animal realms, the human realm, the demi-god realms and the god realms. We cannot physically help to relieve the suffering of most of these boundless beings, so we say prayers for them. But with animals and humans, we can provide actual, physical help. My teacher Kalu Rinpoche was well known for this and was always helping animals. Even while giving teachings, he would be seen simultaneously feeding the many beings around him. He was able to do such a thing because his awareness was vast enough to notice all of these beings needing care. If we pay attention to our surroundings, we notice so many animal beings are constantly around us. We can try not to harm these beings and that is very good. But more than this, we can help these beings. Millions of ants are on the ground. Thousands of birds are flying overhead. Gophers, earthworms, prairie dogs and all kinds of beings are living in the earth. All of them, we can help. We must help them.

Helping beings is an important part of Buddhism. My students and I have even fed the skunks and at one point we even got to feed little baby skunks the size of my hand. There were seven of them. My dear friend Norma asked me to name them and I named them OM, MAN, NI, PAD, MEY, HUNG and HRI. They walked one behind the other, following each other like a spiral in a tornado. It was amazing. I would drop some cat food onto the ground and then they would come and eat it and twirl around and against my legs like a cat would do. I felt very loved and trusted by them. Many people judge skunks because they make a nasty smell. Even just showing some people a photograph of a skunk makes them turn away. However, skunks are peaceful, beautiful animals. Their fart is all they have to protect themselves. They are just trying to find food, shelter and safety like all other animals. In Taos my students and I feed the crows once a week and many birds come to eat. Sometimes 50 crows and ravens fly across the open skies of the Mesa to come and enjoy the food. These are very smart animals. One crow seems to especially enjoy our chanting and comes and sits by the window to listen.

Very few people help animals in this world. Even fewer Buddhist people help animals in this world. Ignoring these beings and having no compassion for them is not Buddhism. We as Buddhists must pay attention to these beings and help them. That is our commitment as Buddhists. We must help if we can.

- *Aaron G.*

Having said these things about helping animals, Lama is also practical. He doesn't ask the impossible. There is always an ongoing debate among Buddhist practitioners about whether or not to eat meat. People who decline to eat meat do so because they do not want a living being to die to make food for them. However, Lama has often pointed out that not eating meat should not make one feel righteous because there are many living beings that die to grow the fruits and the vegetables that feed the non-meat eaters. For instance, there are many bugs and worms that are killed when the land on which these vegetables are grown is plowed and cultivated. Additionally, there are numerous little creatures, often unseen, that die when we step on them as we walk. Here is one student's experience:

One time after our noon potluck during the building of the Kagyu Mila Guru stupa in Questa, I was walking back towards the stupa to return to work. Lama was walking with me. I looked down at the dirt road and noticed a spread-out population of ants covering the entire width of the road. I wondered what I should do about these ants because of our vow not to harm beings. Fortunately, Lama answered my unspoken question. He said, "I just walk as I usually do." How sane. To be a Buddhist I don't need to jump and dance around trying to miss all these barely visible ants. I just need to walk as I usually do. Lama Dorje's statement broke through the kind of minutiae that could have occupied my mind in an unhelpful fashion. It was a blessing for Lama to answer my concern in a straightforward and clear way. Many times since then, this scene comes to mind. With this simple teaching, Lama Dorje encouraged me to be my most functional self in all areas of life. As with many moments with Lama Dorje, this has become a living and on-going teaching for me.

- *Anna R.*

87

Contemplation also gives us time and space to absorb what we have seen or heard. It sharpens our perspective and allows us to see things more clearly and in greater depth. Sometimes it is described as the practice of "being fully present." But while being fully present is the beginning, contemplation reaches its full potential when we examine our thoughts and our experiences without judgment or critique. It is a kind of deep listening to the messages of our hearts and our soul. This is how we come to love things in themselves and for themselves.

WISDOM

Ah! Wisdom, at last. Wisdom, that long sought-after, long desired attribute. Wisdom, the fruit of the tree of patience, diligence and contemplation. Wisdom, the icing on the cake! Wisdom! So, what exactly is Wisdom? It is not merely the accumulation of knowledge, although knowledge helps inform wisdom. It is not what we think of as worldly intelligence, although intelligent action is an important support of wisdom. Wisdom is something else. We know that when we light a fire on the stove, we feel heat. We know that if we place a pot of water on this fire, it will transfer this heat into the water. Embraced by time, this heated water will start to boil and release a totally new substance called steam. Wisdom is somewhat like this. If we take the knowledge we have acquired and combine it with intelligent action, in time, the steam of wisdom will begin to arise.

Wisdom is a special type of understanding. It allows us to separate virtuous action from non-virtuous action. It allows us to know when to act or even if we should act. For example, parents of young children are often confronted with this type of decision. They may watch their young child trying to climb a "jungle gym." These structures are often found in parks and playgrounds and are constructed out of heavy metal climbing bars rising higher and higher into the air. The young child sees the challenge and tries to take it, climbing ever higher on the bars. The watchful parent is confronted with a choice of when and whether to intercede. Obviously, the parent wants to protect the child from injury but at the same time wants to support and encourage the young child's confidence to try new and higher challenges. So, the knowledge of the challenges that the climbing bars present as well as the intellectual understanding of the child's need to develop confidence must be weighed and balanced in the parent's cauldron of wisdom to determine if and when to act.

But wisdom in the context of spiritual life and spiritual practice has another layer. The questions of when to act and how to act are shaped by "why" we act. In the example of the parent and child, the "why" to act is clear. The parent acts because of the care and concern for the child's welfare. This care and concern, this tempered action, is imbued with compassion. It is said that the Buddha did not teach for some time after his enlightenment but remained in the forest in silence. Brahma and Indra reminded him that he had originally vowed to attain enlightenment for the sake of all living beings. Thus, the Buddha began teaching. Having attained enlightenment, the Buddha knew clearly when and how to act, but his teaching came alive with the fire of compassion to bring all beings to enlightenment.

Lama Dorje is masterful in this aspect of teaching. He is rarely concerned with lengthy analyses of the intellectual background of Buddhist concepts. This is certainly not because of a lack of knowledge on his part. His knowledge is extremely profound and when questioned or called upon to speak to such issues, no stone is left unturned. But just because he can speak to these analytical questions does not mean that he will speak. Lama Dorje is very experienced with the Western mind. He knows that we crave accumulation, not only of physical things but mental things as well. His goal is not to fill our minds. His goal is to lead us on the spiritual path to higher wisdom and compassion.

Lama Dorje's teaching style is simple and direct. He does not often engage in lengthy, philosophical discussions. As one student described it:

> *Lama has a few pithy statements that can be applied to life:*
> *"Let them."*
> *"Better than nothing"*
> *"Maybe next time"*
> *These are examples of his all-encompassing wisdom. Lama Dorje*
> *is indeed the Buddha in form.*
>
> - *Rachel S.*

It has been said that knowledge can be imparted to another person but wisdom must be learned and experienced from within. Sometimes the experience of wisdom can come naturally over time based on the gradual accumulation of many smaller experiences. But sometimes there are dramatic, cataclysmic experiences that accelerate the acquisition of wisdom. For example, consider the experience of teaching a small child the consequences of touching a hot stove. You can describe what this intense heat feels like. You can show the child pictures of what fire looks like. You can even gently and cautiously take the child's hand close enough to a burner to feel the heat. This may or may not teach the child not to touch the hot stove. Many of us had to learn the hard way. We had to actually touch the stove, get burned and cry our eyes out because of the pain.

Wise teachers are well aware of this "learn by touching" phenomenon. And as painful as this experience can be, it is rarely a lesson we forget. In truth, it quickly takes us well beyond any intellectual discussion of a hot stove. Lama Dorje is one of the kindest people I have ever met. Yet, he is quite capable of breaking through our intellectual logic when he deems it necessary. And even though we have talked about Lama as a trickster, Lama is quite capable of delivering a "spear to the heart" when this kind of instruction is needed. More accurately, it is not so much a spear to the "heart" as it is a spear to the "ego." I have experienced this more than once from Lama as I have an ego that definitely needs taming! For example, after we had finished building the KMG stupa in Questa, several well-respected, highly regarded Lama's arrived to consecrate the building. Coordination of that event required an enormous amount of effort. Many of the people involved with building the stupa spent countless hours preparing for the event. Since I was one of the coordinators, I had certainly put in my share of effort. To graphically illustrate what I mean, I myself made 13 large pans of lasagna to help feed the crowd! After it was over and I had returned to my home in Santa Fe, I was pleased and relieved that things had gone well. I was pleased with the outcomes of our efforts, but I was also extremely tired. I went out to the stupa to take some things to Lama Dorje and he invited me into his hut and fixed me a lovely cup of tea. Once we were sitting comfortably and I was relaxed and sipping on my tea, Lama Dorje suddenly addressed me quite sternly. He said,

> *You no special. Oh, you think you did all these things for the consecration, and everyone say to you what a good job you did. How wonderful the consecration was. They say your work was really wonderful. But you no special. You just like everyone else.*

He said more things after that which I cannot recall because I was in such shock by those few words. The rest of the conversation became a blur. And my reaction was not noble! Although I maintained a civilized outward demeanor, my interior self was raging! I wanted to cry but I knew from past experience with Lama that crying would make me look like a "crazy" person. I held my tears and I held my temper! I was so emotional that

I could not even attempt to try to see the lesson in his teaching. I left his house and as soon as I was in my car, I cried all the way home. In fact, I cried for days afterward. I said to myself, "*I am done. I am never going to meditation practice again. If this is what Buddhism is about, I want no part of it!*" And, although it is now somewhat embarrassing to admit, I was self-righteously angry with Lama Dorje! "*How could he do this to me? He knew how hard I worked! He knew! And still he could say such a hurtful thing to me!*" It wasn't so much that I expected to be treated in a "special" way but a simple "*Thank You*" would have been nice. But no thank you did I receive from him. Only a strong admonition that I was not special!!

In my righteous indignation, I promised myself that I was not going back to meditation at the stupa. After all, why go to a place that treated me so badly? Why go to a place that valued me so little? Then the time came for the next meditation practice and I felt a dilemma. If I did not go back to practice, Lama could say to all the others, "*Well ... see how strong her commitment is? One small bump in the road and she is gone.*" On the other hand, I was stubborn. I did not want to be so wrongly represented. If I went to the meditation, I could show Lama how wrong he was. I could show him that what he said simply didn't matter. So back I went. But not surprisingly, I was wrong on every count! As I sat on my meditation cushion, I cried my way through the entire practice. Not big, sobbing tears but a steady stream of moisture down my cheeks and out of my nose. And so it continued for the next several practices until one day, I finally got it! I finally began to understand what Lama said and why he said it. The lesson goes something like this:

> If people say nice things about you, it feels good ... and so you spend your time trying to do the things that will make people say more nice things, which is what you want to hear. This may sound nice, but in truth it becomes a prison. None of us do the "right" things all the time. None of us always knows what those "right things" are. But we are doing those things because we want the responses to stroke our ego. This may not always be the "right" thing to do or the most beneficial thing to do. It becomes merely the thing to do to get our ego stroked. It is far better and much wiser to look for deeper motivation.

And so slowly I began to understand both the wisdom and the kindness of Lama's teaching for me. A spear to the heart or a spear to the ego?

Another student of Lama's shares a similar story. David, one of Lama Dorje's Chief Builders, was doing some major construction for Lama in Santa Fe at the KSK Center. He was making badly needed repairs and remodeling an old house that the Center rented out for income. While he was working, Lama came over and talked to him about building a mediation table that Lama needed. David stopped what he was doing and talked to Lama about what he needed and the measurements required for the table. He immediately began working on the table in order to finish it as quickly as possible. And then they stopped for lunch. And that is where things changed. David describes it this way:

> *There were several other people there including Virginia, a long-time student of Lama Dorje whom David also knew well. Virginia and the other people there started thanking David for the work he was doing and telling him how impressed they were with his commitment to helping Lama with various Dharma building projects. Suddenly, Lama Dorje spoke up and said, " The difference between David and me is that David works for himself and I work for all beings." This was like a spear to my heart. I was working really hard and he says that I am not working for all beings!! Everyone in the room felt the tension ... felt the energy.*

But then the story took a strange twist.

> *I left the room and went back to working on the table when I felt something was wrong. Virginia came rushing out to find me and said that Lama Dorje had passed out. We called 911 and the ambulance shows up. I am still not clear about what exactly was going on. The paramedics wanted to take Lama to the hospital, but he refused to go. The paramedics told him that if he didn't go to the hospital, he was going to die. But he still said no. The paramedics said that so long as he was conscious, they could not take him to the hospital if he was refusing to go. They said that so long as he is conscious, then he can decide. I wanted him to go to the hospital but they said we couldn't force him to go. I wasn't really trying to force him, but I just didn't know what was the right thing to do. I knew Lama well enough to know that once he has made a decision, he is not going to change it.*
> *Between Lama's "spear to the heart" and then his apparent brush with death, I suddenly felt very sick. I wanted to go to the bookstore and lie down but the others told me I needed to lie down in the living room next*

to Lama's room because they felt it was unsafe to leave him alone. So I did that ...and I was really sick. I had a bad headache and a fever ... and then I fell asleep. When I woke up, it was suddenly all over. Aaron, another student of Lama Dorje's was there, and he said Lama was feeling much better and when I saw Lama he seemed quite fine. It was as if nothing had ever happened. And suddenly, the spear to my heart was gone.

Wisdom, however learned or however acquired, is a gift. In spite of the severe appearance of his words and actions, Lama Dorje was able to impart wisdom that might never have come otherwise. And his actions, however harsh they may have seemed on the surface, were a great and swift gift.

It is worthwhile to consider the perceptions of others. A longtime student of Lama Dorje's says the following:

> *Lama is truly an enlightened being. His teachings are profound and even devastating for someone like me who tends to rely on my own selfish tendencies in this life! I cannot think of anyone who has shown more kindness ... not kindness in the western sense, but true kindness in the sense of moving one along the path to enlightenment. Lama teaches at a deep level the meaning and fundamental path of Buddhism. Lama's mirror-like mind continues to shine and reveal the truth, disturbing the illusory nature of our actions. For this, I am thankful. Deep vows and prayers for his longevity.*
>
> - *Paul S.*

While knowledge can sometimes be imparted and learned, wisdom must be experienced. Wisdom is not sophisticated, intellectual concepts nor theoretical philosophy. These may inform wisdom but they do not convey it. A teacher with the skill and care to point out our weaknesses and shortcomings and to do so in a skillful way is not an enemy but a blessing. Wisdom is the gift of a true teacher.

LAMA DORJE
MASTER BUILDER

LAMA DORJE – Master Builder

I believe it is somewhat accurate to say that some of Lama Dorje's happiest moments are when he is building. And what a builder he is! During his lifetime, in addition to his many teaching and administrative responsibilities running Dharma centers, Lama Dorje orchestrated and participated in the building of at least four stupas in the following places:

1. Kagyu Shenpen Kunchab Center in Santa Fe, New Mexico,
2. Kagyu Dechen Choling Center in Taos, New Mexico,
3. The Kagyu Mila Guru Center in Questa, New Mexico, and
4. The Kyang Tsik Chorten in Questa, New Mexico

In addition, he offered his knowledge and advice on the building of the Karma Thegsum Tashi Gomang stupa in Crestone, Colorado. He also advised and helped in the building of a private stupa in Santa Fe, New Mexico to commemorate the life and work of Chagdud Tulku, one of the first lamas to visit in the Santa Fe area.

The Kagyu Shenpen Kunchab (KSK) Tibetan Buddhist Center was founded in Santa Fe in 1975 by His Eminence Kalu Rinpoche. Rinpoche wanted to bring the profound teachings of Tibetan Buddhism to some of his earliest students who lived in New Mexico. In 1981, Rinpoche sent Lama Karma Dorje to Santa Fe to be the resident Lama and guide the development of the KSK Center. His Eminence Kalu Rinpoche returned to Santa Fe in 1983 and inspired his students to begin construction of the KSK Stupa under the direction of Lama Dorje and Jeremy Morrell, a local practitioner and skilled carpenter. The Venerable Lama Karma Dorje brought with him from Sikkim a precious text on the proportions of the stupa. Beginning with a mere $2,000, the stupa project quickly gathered momentum. Contributions were given by many people who donated time, money, and materials during the next three years of construction and created not only a wonderful stupa but developed a wonderful group spirit and community.

Readers may ask, "*What is a stupa?*" The answer is both simple and complex. A stupa is an important form of Buddhist architecture. At its simplest, a stupa is a dirt burial mound faced with stone. In fact, the word "*stupa*" is a Sanskrit word meaning "heap". In Buddhism, the earliest stupas contained portions of the Buddha's ashes, and as a result, the stupa began to be associated with the body of the Buddha. Adding the Buddha's ashes to the mound of dirt activates it with the energy of the Buddha himself. But stupas predate the Buddha. It is written that when Buddha Shakyamuni attained enlightenment, he did so in the presence of a stupa. Since his lifetime, stupas have been built all over the world as representations of his form and memorials to his deeds. The ashes of the Buddha were buried in stupas built at locations associated with important events in the Buddha's life including Lumbini (where he was born), Bodh Gaya (where he achieved Enlightenment), Deer Park at Sarnath (where he preached his first sermon), and Kushingara (where he died). The choice of these sites and others was based on both real and legendary events.[11] Even before Buddhism, great teachers were buried in mounds. Some were cremated, but sometimes they were buried in a seated, meditative position. The mound of earth covered them up. Thus, the domed shape of the stupa came to represent a person seated in meditation much as the Buddha was when he achieved Enlightenment. The base of the stupa represents his crossed legs as he sat in a meditative pose (called *padmasana* or the lotus position). The middle portion is the Buddha's body and the top of the mound, where a pole rises from the apex surrounded by a small fence-like crown, represents his head. The following drawing illustrates the stupa and its symbolism and similarities to the sitting Buddha in a meditative posture.

---

[11] *King Ashoka, who was the first king to embrace Buddhism, ruled over most of the Indian subcontinent from c. 269 - 232 B.C.E. According to legend, it is said that he created 84,000 stupas and divided the Buddha's ashes among them all. While this is probably an exaggeration, it is clear that Ashoka was responsible for building many stupas all over northern India and other territories now known as Nepal, Pakistan, Bangladesh, and Afghanistan. One of Ashoka's goals was to provide new converts with the tools to help with their new faith. In this, Ashoka was following the directions of the Buddha who, prior to his death, directed that stupas should be erected so that "the hearts of many shall be made calm and glad." The practice of building stupas spread to Nepal and Tibet, Bhutan, Thailand, Burma, China and even the United States. Stupas remind the Buddhist practitioner of the Buddha and his teachings.*

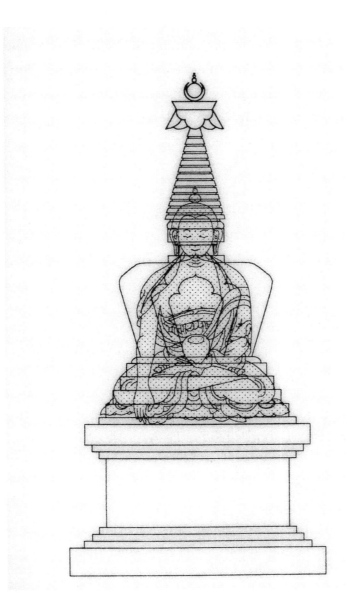

Just as a statue of the Buddha represents the Body of the Buddha and the Dharma texts represent the Speech of the Buddha, a stupa represents the Mind of the Buddha. When built according to correct proportions and when consecrated by a qualified Lama, a stupa becomes literally the Mind of the Buddha and an object of Refuge.

For Buddhists, building stupas also has karmic benefits. Karma, a key component in both Hinduism and Buddhism, is the energy generated by a person's actions and the ethical consequences of those actions. It is similar to the Christian belief that "we reap what we sow." Karma affects a person's next existence or re-birth. For example, in the Buddhist teachings, ten merits of building a stupa are outlined. One of those merits states that if a practitioner builds a stupa, he or she will not be reborn in a remote location and will not suffer from extreme poverty. Buddhists visit stupas to perform rituals that help them to understand the Buddha's teachings. Then when they die, they cease to be caught up in samsara, the endless cycle of birth and death. Once individuals come to fully understand the teachings of the Buddha, they are able to achieve Enlightenment. Buddha means the "Enlightened One." It is the knowledge the Buddha gained on his way to achieving enlightenment that practitioners seek on their own Enlightenment journey.

From this traditional heritage, Lama Dorje began building the KSK Stupa. Other stupas built by and under the direction and guidance of Lama Dorje followed. An article by journalist Anna Racicot appeared in the *New Mexico Magazine* in December of 1998 crediting Lama Dorje's efforts:

> *[The] most well-known known [stupa] is Kagyu Shenpen Kunchab Bodhi Stupa on Airport Road [in Santa Fe, New Mexico]. Finished in 1986 under the direction of Lama Karma Dorje, a native of Sikkim, the Bodhi Stupa is the largest of the state's stupas and contains a spacious shrine room, used several times during the week for Tibetan Buddhist practices or services. Buddhist tradition has it that stupas bless all beings who see them or come in contact with them. Anyone visiting Shenpen Kunchab Bodhi Stupa with its high white walls enclosing quiet gardens, a lotus pond and the majestic stupa, might certainly attest to this. Entering the shrine room, with its exquisitely painted traditional Tibetan designs, fills the viewer with a peace totally unexpected for a place a few minutes off of Cerrillos Road, Santa Fe's busiest thoroughfare.*

Another article by Racicot, entitled *Stupas Along the Rio Grande*, appeared in *Tricycle, A Buddhist Review*. This magazine, with national and international distribution, describes the phenomenon of Tibetan-style stupas that were built along the Rio Grande River. The article states:

> From 1983 to 1996, six Tibetan-style stupas were built in a line roughly following the Rio Grande River from Albuquerque, New Mexico, north to Crestone, Colorado.

As the article further notes:

> Lama Karma Dorje initiated, advised, supervised, and gave direct, hands-on instruction in the building of three of these stupas: 1) the Kagyu Shenpen Kunchab stupa in Santa Fe, New Mexico, 2) the Kagyu Dekyi Choling stupa in Taos, New Mexico, and 3) the Kagyu Mila Guru stupa near Questa, New Mexico.

Lama Dorje also consulted and advised on the building of the Ngagpa Yeshe Dorje stupa on private land in Santa Fe, New Mexico, the Tashi Gomang stupa in Crestone, Colorado and the Kyang Tsik Chorten in Questa, New Mexico.

But Lama's building endeavors were not limited to stupas alone. He organized, designed and participated actively in the building of many other buildings at his various centers. When the KSK Center purchased the property where it now is situated, there were several old and decrepit, small structures on the property. Lama went to work immediately to repair these structures to make them habitable. Partly, this activity was necessary in order for Lama to have a place to live. He repaired a small adobe structure, probably no more than 250 square feet in total, into a livable "hut" for himself. The hut had a bedroom, a small kitchen/living area and a small bathroom. He lived in this structure for over 15 years where he tended to the needs of students, visitors and workers on the property. His hospitality far exceeded the small boundaries of this little hut and many who were fortunate to visit Lama here retain those times fondly in their memories. One could never visit Lama without being offered a cup of Lama's wonderful *chai* (Tibetan tea)!

From his hut, Lama moved forward to repair several more of the old buildings on the property to make them into rentable dwelling spaces. These rentals became the

Center's first source of income for the property. With repairs and additions, they provided a steady source of income that continues today. After these apartments, Lama continued his building activity to repair the largest structure on the property. It was turned into a Guest House that could accommodate visiting Lamas and their entourages. This house contained one large bedroom and three smaller ones, along with a living room large enough to accommodate small groups, a kitchen and bathrooms. This structure turned into a hub of activity as the KSK Stupa was being built. Many of the Lamas and students who arrived to help with the stupa project stayed in this Guest House.

Another of Lama's building projects at KSK was repairing one of the old structures and turning it into a bookstore. Buddhist practitioners could now obtain various Dharma texts and materials to facilitate their practice. Today many of these items are readily accessible through the internet. In the early '80s, however, sources for these materials were difficult to find, especially from a small village in the heart of rural New Mexico. Of course, the heart of Lama's building activity at the KSK Center was the building of its magnificent stupa. But Lama Dorje's building activities were not limited to the KSK Center in Santa Fe. As you continue to read, you will learn about the Centers he established and the Stupas he built in several different areas in northern New Mexico. And as those who were fortunate enough to work with Lama on these endeavors will tell you, even today these are some of the highest and most meaningful experiences of their lives.

Bear in mind that these many building projects were not the result of great donations of money from single individuals. No, these projects were built with many modest donations of time and materials and money given over the course of time. Lama's building mantra was something like, *"If you start to build it, the money will come."* And that is exactly what happened. That is the way that most of Lama's building activities were funded.

But the less obvious source of "funding" was Lama himself. His enthusiasm and his selfless commitment made you want to help, made you want to find the time to work on one of the building projects, made you want to stretch your checkbook to make a small donation to help build, and made you want to buy a bag of cement to donate to the building effort. Something about Lama and his joyful energy and deep commitment to helping bring goodness into the world made you want to contribute the best you had to offer. You didn't do it because he asked you to. You didn't do it because you felt you should. You did it because you genuinely and honestly wanted to. And your reward was not a personal *"Thank You"* note nor an engraved plaque. Your reward was a deep feeling of meaning and purpose that inspired you to reach higher.

KAGYU SHENPEN KUNCHAB STUPA

SANTA FE, NEW MEXICO

KAGYU SHENPEN KUNCHAB

The KSK Tibetan Buddhist Center had its earliest beginnings in the home of Ken and Sally Maynard who lived on Irvine Street in Santa Fe, New Mexico. When he first came to Santa Fe, Lama Dorje lived with Ken and Sally Maynard on Irvine Street until land for the KSK Center was purchased on Airport Road on the southwest side of the city. At that time, Airport Road was a small two-lane road with little development and almost no commercial activity. The property purchased was about 2 acres and had several small old adobes in decrepit condition on the property. Lama's first project was to make some of these houses habitable. He saw these early projects as necessary for several reasons. First, he needed a place to live, and second, if some of these same dwellings could be made habitable, they could be rented out and thereby establish an income flow for the Center. In fact, from those early days to the present, the rental units on the property have remained a major source of income for the KSK Center. This foresight exemplifies Lama's keen business sense and great mathematical mind. These early projects then set the stage for the building of the KSK Stupa.

By way of background, the Kagyu Shenpen Kunchab Tibetan Buddhist Center was founded in Santa Fe in 1975 by His Eminence Kalu Rinpoche to bring the profound teachings of Tibetan Buddhism to New Mexico. In 1981, Kalu Rinpoche sent Lama Karma Dorje to Santa Fe to become a resident teacher for this small group of Rinpoche's students and to establish a Karma Kagyu dharma center. In 1983 His Eminence Kalu Rinpoche returned to Santa Fe, inspiring his students to begin construction of the KSK Stupa under the direction of Lama Dorje and Jeremy(Jerry) Morrell, a local practitioner and skilled carpenter. Morrell had built other Tibetan Buddhist buildings including a retreat center for Kalu Rinpoche in France. The Venerable Lama Karma Dorje brought with him from Sikkim a precious text on the proportions of the stupa. Describing the KSK stupa, Morrell said:

Although the size of Tibetan Buddhist chapels may vary, the proportions are absolutely critical. They've never varied in over 2,500 years, since the first one appeared in the sky during the time of Buddha. The average stupa is around 35 feet high and has a solid base. The KSK stupa will have a vaulted-ceiling room inside for religious ceremonies. ... a rarity for a stupa. Only a handful in the world have this feature. Inside, the room will focus a life-sized statue of Buddha and a thousand, 8-inch high Buddhas will line the wall of the chamber.

The inside of the stupa was also designed to hold what is called the *Kangyur*, the entire canon of Tibetan Buddhism in its original language, a collection of 108 volumes. The stupa was designed to be a *bodhi* or enlightenment stupa, symbolizing Buddha's final enlightenment and absolute purity. Anticipating how the work of this stupa would be accomplished, Morrell said:

"Nearly all of the work on this stupa will be done by center members. We may hire a structural contractor, but most of the work we definitely intend to do ourselves."

The building of the stupa was a little more complicated than originally anticipated. Beginning with a mere $2,000, the stupa project quickly gathered momentum. Contributions were given by many people who donated time, money, and materials during the next three years of construction and created not only a wonderful stupa but developed a wonderful group spirit and sangha. The Venerable Deshung Rinpoche donated jewel vases that were buried under the foundation. The Venerable Chagdud Rinpoche visited and sculpted the life-size Buddha statue. Various artists, under the direction of Lama Dorje, Sanje Elliot and Cynthia Moku, painted murals depicting the lineages, deities and thousand Buddhas of the eon that are painted on the interior of the stupa walls. In 1986 His Eminence Kalu Rinpoche returned, bringing with him a pearl-like crystal that had been recovered from the cremation of Buddha Shakyamuni. This crystal was one of the treasures placed inside the stupa during construction.

So, against this rich background, the KSK Stupa was built. It is a large and imposing structure, reaching 65 feet in the sky with a spire ornamented by its golden crown and nestled strikingly against the clear blue New Mexico sky. Below the spire, a Buddha statue is set into a large alcove and easily seen from some distance away. A long, tapered pillar of wood lacquered with red and embellished with Tibetan mantras in gold letters, called in Tibetan a *tsog shing,* was installed in the spire. With a touch of irony, this beautiful stupa sits next to a trailer park on what has become one of the busiest roads in Santa Fe.

Under the direction of Lama Dorje and working closely with Jerry Morell, the building of the stupa took three years, with help on the weekends from members of the Santa Fe sangha. The stupa's serene, white painted exterior is highlighted with red doors and blue woodwork decorated with lotus designs in gold paint. Originally planned as a small, solid structure about 15 feet high, it evolved into the present form which is 65 feet high on a 30-foot square base. The stupa was built with modern, reinforced concrete techniques requiring 210 tons of concrete and untold amounts of rebar. It took approximately 60,000 hours of donated labor and about $75,000 worth of material to build. It is indicative of the tremendous energy and inspiration of Kalu Rinpoche, Lama Karma Dorje and their students that a project of this magnitude could be undertaken and completed by a sangha of less than 20 members and perhaps twice as many volunteers.

But the beautiful exterior of the stupa is only a prelude of the beauty inside. As one enters this stupa through the dramatic red doors on the North side, one is completely overwhelmed by the numerous and exquisitely detailed paintings of the various deities in the Tibetan Buddhist tradition. You immediately face the South wall with a large statue of Shakyamuni Buddha sitting in the middle that was crafted by the Venerable Chagdud Tulku. The Buddha sits above the magnificent altar containing many offering bowls and beautifully sculpted torma offerings. The central Buddha is surrounded by a hundred smaller, gold Buddha statues, exemplifying the all-pervasive presence of Buddha nature.

. On the West wall of the shrine room, to the right of the Buddha, are paintings of the Five Buddha families. The Karma Kagyu Lineage is represented on the West wall with paintings of Tilopa, Naropa, Marpa , Milarepa and Gampopa. The primary figure on the West Wall is Chenrezig (Avilokiteshvara), Lord of Compassion and a deity much revered in the Tibetan Buddhist tradition. To the left of the Buddha on the East wall are representations of the Shangpa Kagyu lineage, along with Green Tara, the female Bodhisattva of Compassion, Vajrasattva (Dorje Sempa) and Vajrayogini. The paintings on the North Wall represent many of the protective deities in the Tibetan tradition including the Bodhisattvas Manjushri [wisdom], Vajrapani [power], and Avalokitesvara [compassion]. [12]

The consecration of the KSK stupa was completed on November 23, 1986, by His Eminence Kalu Rinpoche on his last visit to New Mexico. Under the kind and vigilant care of Lama Karma Dorje, the KSK Center has flourished over the intervening years and has hosted teachers of all the major lineages of Tibetan Buddhism as well as the His Holiness, the Dalai Lama. Under forty years of Lama Karma Dorje's direction, the KSK Center continues to this day as a thriving Tibetan center and community.

---

[12] *A detailed description of the paintings in the shrine room of the KSK Stupa is contained in the Appendices.*

**ALTAR ON SOUTH WALL
INSIDE STUPA**

**EAST WALL ON
INSIDE OF KSK STUPA**

**WEST WALL ON
INSIDE OF KSK STUPA**

LAMA DORJE SAYS PRAYERS FOR THE BIRD

**SNOW BRINGS AUSPICIOUS
BLESSING TO THE STUPA**

KAGYU DEKYI CHOLING STUPA

TRES OREJAS (TAOS), NEW MEXICO

KAGYU DEKYI CHOLING

About 8 miles northwest of Taos, New Mexico, and about two miles from the western rim of the Rio Grande Gorge, sits a mountain range known as Tres Orejas. The name, which means "three ears", accurately describes this range. In profile, there are three peaks, looking very similar in shape to an ear lying on its side. The views eastward from Tres Orejas of the Taos Valley are nothing short of spectacular. There are views of sacred Taos Mountain and Truchas Peaks as they lay nestled in the southern tip of the Sangre de Cristo Mountain range. The land, covered with sagebrush, chamisa and pinon trees, has an interesting history. In the late 1960s, an ambitious land speculator bought a wide expanse of this land, divided it into lots and sold the parcels to people all over the country, most of whom bought the property sight unseen. While offering incredible views, the land had one serious flaw. There was no water on the property, which is not an uncommon situation in the high desert country of northern New Mexico. As the unsuspecting purchasers of these land parcels soon discovered, this lack of water made the property unsuitable for building. Following this discovery, most of the owners of these parcels stopped paying the taxes on the property and the parcels were forfeited for failure to pay.

Over time, these parcels were sold for modest amounts to those willing to pay the back taxes that were owed. The new purchasers of these land parcels were folks of lesser means who were well aware of the challenges faced by the lack of water. However, what these new purchasers may have lacked in money was more than compensated by their innovative building methods and clever uses of the land. They were not interested in the amenities offered by modern, suburban households but more interested in the solitude and back-to-earth living that this area afforded. In time, the loosely formed community, now known as Tres Orejas, developed.

In this unique community of Tres Orejas, Kagyu Dekyi Choling Buddhist Center was established. The genesis of this stupa and center is a sweet story. It is a story of kindness and friendship between Lama Dorje and Norbert Ubechel, a student of Lama

Dorje. Norbert was very young at the time of their meeting. He was in his early twenties and had a young wife. They were in San Francisco and had met Lama Lodrö who had a Tibetan Buddhist Center there on Fell Street. Lama Lodrö told Norbert that there was also a Tibetan Buddhist Center in Santa Fe, New Mexico. Combining the innocence of his youth with an adventuresome spirit, Norbert and his wife left San Francisco and headed toward Santa Fe. Norbert's resources were slim but he followed his heart and made the journey.

He arrived in Santa Fe with no known acquaintances, no resources and no money. To his great good fortune, upon arriving in Santa Fe, he met Lama Dorje. And Lama Dorje, himself a new arrival in Santa Fe, was moved to help this young man and his wife. Lama Dorje was at that time living with the Maynards in a house on Irvine Street which also was the location of the newly formed KSK Center. Lama Dorje, recognizing the rather destitute nature of Norbert's resources, invited Norbert and his wife to stay in one of the rooms at the Center. Lama cooked and prepared food for them. Norbert describes the meeting of these two individuals as follows:

> *This story goes back to 1981. In early September of that year, I came from San Francisco with my new wife. We arrived in Santa Fe and this was before anyone made telephone calls. We went to the Center which at that time was on Irvine Street. Lama Dorje was there and he welcomed us in. Lama did not speak much English but he recognized right away that we neither had money nor a place to stay. We were very very poor! He said, you can come here and you can stay here with me and Ken and Sally. He gave us a room where we could stay and Lama cooked and hosted and always fed us. He was so very kind.*

And in his not surprising but practical fashion, Lama Dorje told Norbert that he needed to find a job. Lama had been in the U.S. long enough to know that survival here required more than desire, it also required cash! Norbert says:

> *He realized that I needed to find a job and he said you go and find a job. He talked to Jerry Morell and Jerry said I have a job and you can come with me. So I got my first job through Lama Dorje. We stayed at the center for 2 or 3 weeks and then we found a place near Penasco in Chamisal. We moved up there. It was very primitive ... an old farmhouse*

about a mile from anything and we stayed there. It had no running water. We got this house and Lama came up shortly after we moved in there and he brought us groceries. In fact, he came up every week for several months and brought us bags of groceries. I was very thankful. He was very concerned and kept track of our lives. He really helped us out.

In many ways, this is classic Lama Dorje. Although he has very little, he is always willing to share and help others. And he shares without judgment. He doesn't arbitrarily decide this person needs help or this person is not worthy of helping. No, he helps where he perceives help is needed. Remember, Lama was quite poor himself. He had come to Santa Fe from Los Angeles only months before. And recall that during his "being lost" adventure, he tried to give the FBI person money and showed him his money bag which he had tied around his waist. The bag contained 100 dollars in American money. Lama told the FBI man that this was money that he exchanged from Indian rupees into American dollars before he left Sikkim. Even in America in 1981, this was not a huge amount of money. Nonetheless, Lama offered whatever he had to help Norbert and his wife. He even brought them groceries to their house in Chamisal, a small town in Northern New Mexico about 50 miles from Santa Fe.

But before long, circumstances started to change for Norbert. His wife became pregnant, and he saw the need to move closer to town. So, they moved to Taos where Norbert got a job working at Taos Ski Valley. It was during this time that Norbert bought some land. He purchased his first lot in Tres Orejas. At that time there was hardly anyone living in that area.

Norbert wanted to have a Thanksgiving celebration and Lama came for his first visit to Tres Orejas. Ken and Sally Maynard brought him from Santa Fe, but the road was so heavy with snow that their vehicle could not make it all the way. They parked on the side of the road, about 2 miles from Norbert's house. Lama loved the location of the site and the spectacular view across the Taos Valley. And as Norbert says, the day Lama came to visit, there was about three feet of snow on the ground! But nothing was going to stop Lama Dorje from making it to Norbert's house. So, he walked the entire distance, through three feet of snow, in flip-flops! Norbert remembers:

Then my wife got pregnant and we moved to Taos. I ended up buying one lot in Tres Orejas. The price was cheap and it only cost us the amount of back taxes that had not been paid by the previous landowner. And the first year we had a Thanksgiving celebration. I think that was in 1982. We had a Thanksgiving party and Lama came up with Ken and Sally. And it had snowed ... the snow was about three feet deep. And there were almost no houses up here at that time ... maybe 3 or 4 houses on this entire mesa. Lama came out and he said this is the most beautiful place I have ever seen. I told him, Lama I have this one piece of land here on this hill. If you want it you can have it. That is the place where his house is now.

Lama loved the land in Tres Orejas. In truth, the views there are so majestic it would be hard not to find the land beautiful. Norbert kindly offered Lama one of the lots Norbert had purchased by paying the back taxes on the property. This was also the act of friends helping friends. Lama had generously helped Norbert when he arrived in Santa Fe virtually penniless. And Lama helped without judgment. What Lama saw in Norbert was an individual who needed support and Lama generously responded. And their friendship continued to grow. Norbert says,

To make a long story short, Lama loved it. We decided to build him a cabin. Since Jerry (Morell) was a really good builder, he said to come down to Santa Fe and we will build the entire house and have a fundraiser. So we did this three times and then we built the house. The house we built was really just a large wooden box. It was pretty basic ... just the walls and openings for the doors and windows Then we rented a truck and a trailer and we drove it up here. And it was in pieces. Then in one day, we stood the whole thing up. Over the course of the year, I refined it a little bit and Lama kept coming up often.

And clearly, Lama Dorje loved this place. Undeterred by the extreme conditions, Lama Dorje came to visit. It became a retreat space for him. Even before his little box of a house was built, he traveled to Tres Orejas to do a retreat. At that time there were very few dwellings in that area, but even these houses were unoccupied in the winter because the winter weather could be very severe. Without electricity and water, living in Tres Orejas in the wintertime was very difficult and even potentially dangerous. But Lama

Dorje saw it as the ultimate place of retreat and he was undeterred by the difficulties that awaited him living in Tres Orejas in the winter. So he packed up his meditation texts and a few clothes and headed up to Tres Orejas. Norbert has very vivid memories of that time:

> *But before his house was built, in fact it was 1985 in January or February, right after my son Narayan was born, Lama ended up surprising me and came to my house. We were living in Taos at that time because Suzanne, my wife, didn't want to live out at Tres Orejas because there was no water ... no electricity ... so we stayed in town. Lama came with two very big suitcases ... someone dropped him off ... and he had all these texts and only a few clothes. He surprised me because he came with all his puja books and clothes and he had a bag of rice and something else. I can't remember exactly.*
>
> *He said, "Can you take me out to the mesa to your house?" He wanted to get away from Santa Fe. There was tension there or something and he wanted to get away he said. I told him I did not have a car that could get out there. First, it was very muddy and then there was all this snow. I said I am going to call a friend who has a four-wheel drive vehicle ... that was a big deal back then...and we got as far as the main road at the flag, which was about a mile and a half from my house. Then this friend of ours and Lama Dorje and I started walking carrying jugs of water, food, and Lama's suitcases. It was going kind of slow and I said I am going to run ahead with some of the suitcases or the water. It's a mile and a half and I will get a fire started and we will have lunch or something. It was very, very hard walking through all this snow. There was probably almost three feet of snow on the ground ... and that is hard walking. And as I recall, Lama was walking in flip-flops!*
>
> *So Lama settled into my house. It was vacant then ... it was a dome house ... there were very few things ... there were some candles and a wood stove ... that kind of thing and Lama stayed for a month or 6 weeks. He stayed for quite a while. Since it was winter, the air was very clear. Our way of communicating to see how he was doing was at sunrise. I would drive up onto Blueberry Hill [on the outskirts of Taos] on the west side with a pair of binoculars that my dad had given me and I would wait for the sun to come up over the mountain. When it did, it would shine on Tres Orejas before it would get light in town and I would fix the binoculars and I could see him either walking or praying in the dome. And I would see smoke from the wood stove and then I would know that he was all right.*

I would come out there two or three times and bring him some food and supplies. He was the only person living on the mesa at that time. There was no one living in the other four houses that were out there at that time because without water and electricity living there was very difficult, and the climate was severe. Lama was the only one out there with very limited resources. But I tried to bring him things. Really it was all kind of a scramble. But it was very good ... a very good time.

So, Lama stayed and prayed. And in the coming years, Tres Orejas became a special place for Lama Dorje. His presence attracted people and the beginning of what became the Kagyu Dekyi Choling Tibetan Buddhist Center began. It was here also that the seeds were planted for the building of a stupa. In 1986, His Holiness Kalu Rinpoche visited New Mexico and he traveled from Santa Fe to see Lama's retreat place in Tres Orejas. As Norbert relates, the story of the genesis of the KDC stupa unfolds:

So I think in about 1986 maybe, Kalu Rinpoche came to give two talks at the old white church on Quesnel Street in Taos. The arrangement was that after the talk he was going to come out to Tres Orejas and have lunch at my house... the dome ... on the mesa. By this time, I had done more work on my dome house and it was a suitable place to host Kalu Rinpoche and his entourage. Two friends were there at the time, Michael Thames and my girlfriend, and they were cooking lunch for all the lamas that were coming. I had probably been living in the dome for 5 or 6 years. Kalu Rinpoche came out and it was a very muddy day and we were grinding up the road with all the lamas. Kalu Rinpoche's attendant and Lama Dorje and I were in my car driving towards the airport near the Rio Grande Gorge Bridge, when suddenly two lights of a police car came behind us. And I was driving very fast and I thought he was pulling me over. And Kalu Rinpoche just did a few mantras and the cop turned off the lights and went away. The cop just turned off the lights and went by us!

Then we came out to my house here in Tres Orejas. We came out here and Lama pointed out the piece of land I had given him. It was too muddy to go up here. Then Kalu Rinpoche said some prayers and then he came into the house for dinner. After dinner, he gave me this small stupa as a gift. He said this stupa is for you and the Center and it's a gift for hosting me. He also gave me a Mahakala thangka ... a very old one. The visit with Kalu Rinpoche ended and then a few weeks later Lama Dorje came up and he said, "You know, you accepted the gift of the stupa.

Well, you know what that means?" I said, "No, what does it mean?" He said, "It means that you are going to build a stupa." I said, WOW OK! How does it work?" He said, "we will make it out of concrete... but it is no big deal. It is not a problem." He said, "You can do it." I said, "OK Lama I will do it." But of course, I didn't know how many bags of cement we would use and how much time it would take. But Lama would come up on Saturday all spring, summer and fall and we would work on the stupa. And occasionally, he would come and surprise me in my shop and he would say, "Now you tell your people today that they are coming to work on the stupa!!" And that's how we got started.

So, in 1986, Lama Karma Dorje and his friend and student, Norbert Ubechel, forged their way on the then barely passable dirt roads to carve out of the dust and mud an authentic spiritual refuge. With Lama and Norbert heading up a crew of neighbors and students, Lama's modest retreat house was built, followed by the arduous task of building the KDC Stupa. That stupa, gleaming white and standing about 22 feet high, commands views of unparalleled beauty. It sits atop the Rio Grande Gorge that cuts across the Taos Valley floor, under vast, ever-changing skies, amid forest and sage and wildlife in abundance. Many who come to this place feel like they are transported to Tibet. The gleaming white stupa radiates blessings of peace, harmony, and well-being across the Taos Valley.

Lama says that this stupa is perfectly positioned. It faces east looking at the sacred Taos Mountain and the Truchas Peaks. It rises up not only from the western rim of the Rio Grande River but also from the sacred river that runs through the center of Taos Pueblo coming down from Blue Lake. Lama says there are seven rivers that converge near the location of the stupa. Some are seen and some unseen, which makes this a very special place. Lama says he has been to all of these rivers over the years although some of them are now not open to visitors. Lama says he is sad that they locked off some of the rivers because poor people need water.

But as often happens on Lama Dorje projects, additional help emerged. Construction of any buildings in this area must be done without a natural water supply. The stupa in particular had substantial water requirements in order to mix the concrete and blocks from which the stupa was built. This meant that the working crew on the stupa had to haul water from the Rio Grande ten to twelve miles away to have water available at the building site. Lama Dorje says that Gal, one of his students, very faithfully hauled water every week so that they had plenty of water to mix the cement for the stupa. He did so every week for the three years it took to complete the stupa construction. Norbert describes those times in this way:

> There were lots of people who helped. I did not do this alone... Gal and Janice, Ken McNamara, David Bates. And some people helped build and some people cooked. Different people came. Pam and Cassandra always brought food. Lots of people helped but I was in charge of making the building happen.

David Bates, an experienced builder who remains to this day as one of Lama Dorje's main "go to" builders, came onto the stupa building scene as it was nearing completion. David describes his first meeting of Lama Dorje:

> I had read a book by Thich Nhat Hanh when I was in Costa Rica. He said, "You need a sangha [a spiritual community]." By this time, I had met my wife Cassandra. She and her friend Pam Parker had met Lama Dorje and so we decided to drive out to Tres Orejas so I could meet Lama. As we were driving out to the mesa, I kept getting this feeling of "chill bumps" in my body. I thought to myself, "What is happening?" When we got there, Lama was up there with Norbert and they were working on the porch of the gompa [the meditation hall that they started after the stupa was completed.] I asked, "Lama, can I help you guys?" He said "yes," and handed me a hammer.

After David related this story, I asked him what happened next. He chuckled and said:

> Well, since that time, since 1995 when I first met Lama, I have gone up to Tres Orejas every Saturday, although last year, I took a little sabbatical ... for about three months. Then Lama called me up and said, "It has been about three months," and I said, "I am coming back. I could not abandon Lama. I could not abandon the dharma center."

In truth, one could hardly call David abandoning the Lama or abandoning the center. Since his first meeting with Lama Dorje, he has applied his building skills to many of Lama Dorje's building projects, both at the KDC Center in Taos and KSK Center in Santa Fe. Under Lama's direction, he built retreat houses and constructed a special building to house the sacred Buddhist text called the Kangyur[13]. Along with other helpers, he also fixed Lama's house in Tres Orejas so it was habitable. In Santa Fe David helped Lama rebuild the Lama Guest House at the KSK Center and repainted the large bumpa or dome on the grand stupa. Quite a body of work since Bates first met Lama Dorje in 1995. And, as David says:

> *And from that first time of working with Lama on the day that we met, I have been working with him ever since.*

And "ever since" has been quite a long and productive period of time.

But David acknowledges that some of the greatest teachings he received from Lama Dorje occurred while working side by side with him on these many building projects. David says:

> *When we worked on a project, he always worked right there with us. And it was his energy that somehow kept the project going. I mean we would do things like getting the materials and bringing them to the site, but they might have just sat there if it wasn't for Lama and his energy that kept things moving along. We really couldn't do it without Lama. And we really wouldn't have done it without Lama. I mean, who would do that? Who would work on a Saturday, a worker's normal day off, in the hot New Mexico sun, doing heavy construction work? Who would voluntarily do that? But Lama made that happen and it was OK. We did it! And the reason you want to do it was because Lama was there. When he wasn't there, you felt very different. You started thinking, "Why am I here? Why am I doing this ... working in the hot sun on a Saturday afternoon?" But when Lama was there, it was very different. And it was while we were doing construction work that Lama gave some of his greatest teachings... not in "formal" teachings," but he gave teachings all the time. When we were working and maybe you were trying to find a hammer or something and he would suddenly be telling you something really important ... something really meaningful. I mean he gave*

---

[13] **Kangyur** *or "Translated Words" consists of works in 108 volumes of the complete teachings of the Buddha as they were spoken by the Buddha himself. All texts presumably once had Sanskrit originals, but the Kangyur as we know it today is written in the Tibetan language. Copies of the Kangyur have become extremely rare since many of them were destroyed after the Chinese invaded Tibet.*

teachings all the time. He didn't just say, "Today I am going to teach you about Chenrezig," ... and launch into a discussion about Chenrezig. And then he would say something and when I thought about what he said, I would realize he taught us a lot about Chenrezig. He taught us about the six realms and things like that. Not in the formal sense but the real teachings came when you were working with him.

But how did all this construction work lead into doing actual meditation practice? How did so many of the folks who helped with the construction suddenly start coming out to the Center for weekly mediation? David explains it this way:

Well, I think Lama is a bit of a trickster! Back then, when we were working, they weren't even doing "puja [meditation practice]." We were just building. So we would just go and work. And then Lama started saying, "Well, now we do puja and then we work." And I thought, "Puja? What's that about?" And it was long!!! And then working in the afternoon? Which was kind of brutal because it gets really hot! Then Cassandra and Pam would kind of figure out what the next project would be. They were kind of the local engine that was helping Lama make it happen. They also cooked food for us every week ... that was also persuasive!" And then Lama would give us a little money for materials to kind of keep things going ... just little by little. And he kept the pujas going. We kept doing pujas ... long pujas ... and then doing hard, hot work in the afternoon sun. So he kind of tricked us into going to puja!

And that's the whole thing. I can't even believe I went up there on Saturdays to work in the hot sun after working all week! But it was really Lama Dorje. And people say, "Oh, don't be attached to the teacher" ... but it's hard not to. With someone like Lama Dorje, it's hard not to be attached. In fact, you want to be attached. And you don't really even think of it as being "attached," You just know you want to be around this man.

David's sentiments are echoed time and again by so many of the students of Lama Dorje. Time and again, they would sacrifice to work on a project with Lama. And almost every person would happily do it all again. On August 8, 1994, the Venerable Lama Lodrö consecrated the KDC Stupa. It was later blessed by Yangsi Kalu Rinpoche and Bokar Rinpoche, Masters of the Shangpa Kagyu lineage. But the building at KDC did not stop with the completion of the stupa. The community proceeded to construct two Gompas [meditation halls] and three retreat houses. Norbert says:

Then eventually we bought more land and more land. One of the very stupid things I did was I put the stupa on the wrong piece of land. It was the one piece that wasn't ours! It was almost done when I realized it. It coincided with Lama Yeshe and Lama Tsering coming around. They had been going back and forth between New Mexico and Oregon. And I talked with Yeshe and I said I need to take care of this. I know who the lady is, I know where she lives I researched it all and I need to deal with that. And Yeshe said you know, we are going to come through that neighborhood on our way down from Oregon. She lived in California. Yeshe said, I will give her a call and I said I will exchange any piece of land I have in exchange for her land. She didn't want money, she wanted land. And Yeshe was very helpful. He straightened it out with her. And so I gave her a piece of land.

Then in the mid-90s, after years of searching, Lama Dorje was able to acquire a complete set of the Kangyur, a collection of 108 volumes containing the complete teachings of the Buddha. Copies of the Kangyur are rare, as many of these were destroyed during the Chinese cultural revolution. A building needed to be constructed in which to house the Kangyur and make certain that the texts were protected. Once again, the KDC community put their shoulders to the task and built the "Kangyur House" out of concrete and concrete blocks to assure its longevity. Remember, all this construction took place without either a water supply or electricity. None of this would have been possible without the inspiration and commitment of Lama Karma Dorje, who at every step of the way, worked shoulder to shoulder with the members of the KDC community and volunteers to bring these buildings into form. And amidst the chamisa, the sagebrush, and the waterless landscape, KDC continues to this day to be a dynamic and vital Tibetan Buddhist Center and community.

**KAGYU DECHEN CHOLING Stupa
in Taos. New Mexico**

**LAMA DORJE GETS THE
LAST LAUGH!**

**LAMA DORJE and NORBERT lay out
the foundation for the KDC Stupa**

LAMA LODRÖ CONSECRATES
THE KDC STUPA

VEN. BOKAR RINPOCHE AND
KHENPO DÖNYO VISIT KDC

LAMA DORJE, LAMA CHODRAK,
NORBERT, AMY,
ALICE & GAL

LAMA DORJE RELAXES WITH NORBERT AND GAL AFTER A HARD DAY'S WORK

KDC WORKING CREW

LAMA DORJE SHARES HIS FEAST OFFERING WITH VIRGINIA

KDC GOMPA MEDITATION BUILDING

KDC GOMPA WITH PRAYER WHEELS
NESTLED IN THE QUIET HILLS
CALLED TRES OREJAS

APPROACHING THE DOORS TO THE GOMPA

**KANGYUR HOUSE
LOOKING OUT OVER THE
BEAUTIFUL TAOS VALLEY**

**MAGNIFICENT VIEWS OF
THE TAOS VALLEY FROM KDC STUPA**

KAGYU DEKYI CHOLING STUPA

KAGYU MILA GURU STUPA

QUESTA, NEW MEXICO

KAGYU MILA GURU STUPA

Nestled in the foothills on the northern end of the Sangre de Christo mountains, about eight miles north of Questa, New Mexico, is a lovely and long-established community of spiritual seekers known as Lorien. Lorien had its genesis under the guidance of Herman Rednick, who was both an accomplished artist and an authentic spiritual teacher. Until his death in 1985, Herman taught and counseled a group of students who gradually came to build their own homes and settle in the Lorien community. Several years after Herman's death, some of his students came to know and appreciate Lama Karma Dorje at the KSK Tibetan Buddhist Center in Santa Fe. They invited Lama Dorje to visit Lorien and to talk with the students there. Many in the Lorien community came to value Lama Dorje's teachings and asked him to visit on a regular basis, which he agreed to do.

So periodically over the next year, Lama Dorje's students in Santa Fe would drive Lama up to Lorien for teachings. I happen to have been one of those students. The other accompanying student was Virginia Oppenheimer, another student of Lama Dorje's and a long-time friend of mine and Dharma sister. The drive from Santa Fe to Lorien was about a 3-hour drive. We would leave Santa Fe at 7 o'clock in the morning and arrive in Lorien around 10 o'clock. Lama would then lead a meditation in the Herman Rednick Center followed by a question-and-answer period. Lama answered questions about Buddhism, in particular, and spiritual life, in general. The meditation period was followed by a potluck luncheon where folks got to talk and exchange stories and events with Lama. Lama came to understand quite deeply and sincerely the commitments and aspirations of these spiritual practitioners. Lama also got to walk around the land and various buildings owned by the organization called Earth Journey. Earth Journey is a non-profit corporation that manages the land and buildings it owns in the Lorien community.

Around this same time, in November of 1991, my mother, who lived in North Carolina, died from cancer. I went back to North Carolina to be with my brothers and sister and to help care for our mother in her final days. After Mom's death, she left each of her children a sum of money. As I was flying back from North Carolina after her funeral to my home in Santa Fe, I was quite naturally thinking about my mother and what a wonderful and strong influence she had been in my life. I wondered what I could do to commemorate her in a special way. As the plane flew over the Sandia mountains east of Albuquerque preparing its descent into the airport, I suddenly realized that what I wanted to do was build a small stupa in her honor on some land that I owned in Lorien. The idea was crystal clear. I knew I could not build a stupa on my own and needed to discuss my idea with Lama Dorje. I drove straight from the airport to Lama Dorje's house at the KSK Center in Santa Fe.

Lama greeted me with a cup of tea, and I talked with him about my idea. His response was positive, and he said that he would help me. Bear in mind, that at this point, my thoughts were to build a small stupa, as I knew that I would need to hire someone to build it and that my funds were insufficient to cover anything larger than a stupa maybe 5 or 6 feet high. Lama and I discussed talking to Charles Dillon, a long-time friend who had been a student of Herman's and was also a general contractor. I called Charles and we arranged to have lunch together on his next trip down to Santa Fe. Over a delightful Japanese meal of sushi and rice, I discussed my idea about the stupa with Charles. I was somewhat apprehensive about his reaction because building a stupa was an unusual request. Charles not only liked my idea but was immediately excited about the project. We continued to talk and then we talked with Lama Dorje. Lama Dorje suggested that we talk with the Lorien community about the plan. So, we did. And the reaction from the community was totally overwhelming. Everyone was excited, but they did not want to build the small 6-foot stupa I had envisioned. They wanted to build a "real" sized stupa! I liked that idea as well but wondered where we would get the money for such a project. Lama Dorje said, *"If you start to build, the money will come!"*

Plans were drawn up and presented to the community. Everyone was excited except the children! They liked the stupa idea but wanted us to build a stupa that you could go inside! We knew that such a design would take even more money to build than a solid stupa, but the children were adamant. I agreed to take their idea back to Lama Dorje and see what he had to say. That very day, I drove back to Santa Fe and went straight out to the KSK Center to talk with Lama. I told him about the children's request, and he said, *"If the children want, then we must do!"* And do we did.

Additionally, Jane Lipman, another one of Herman's students who owned land adjacent to mine, offered to have the stupa built on her land. This was a most generous offer and we accepted it gratefully. Not only did Jane offer the land on which to build the stupa but she offered an entire 5-acre parcel which created space not only for the stupa but for retreat cabins and bathroom facilities that were built later after the stupa was completed.

I cannot begin to describe the joy that building this stupa gave. It may sound unbelievable that driving five or six hours every Saturday to go to a chamisa-filled site and mix concrete with a hoe in a wheelbarrow or dig foundations in the hard dry soil was a joyful event, but it was. We had a steady group of hard-working people who showed up and worked diligently with few complaints and lots of fun. In the Acknowledgements section of this book, I have included the names of the inner core of workers on this stupa and a word or two about their background. We also had children who came to work and seemed as excited about building the stupa as the adults.

Speaking of the children, it was heartwarming to see how Lama Dorje related to the children and they with him. He actually taught them some building techniques with piles of sticks and dirt. Lama has a way with children that is beautiful to watch. In the intervening years, he continued advising these same children as they became young adults.

And from humble beginnings, the money for the stupa grew as needed at every stage of the construction. Donations ranged from low to high but most were as modest as most people's budgets would allow. Lama advised us not to worry. He often said, *"Five dollars will buy another bag of cement."* And so it did. And it was with these donations and the many bags of concrete that they bought that the Kagyu Mila Guru stupa was completed and consecrated in 1994, three years after it was started.

139

The consecration of the stupa in 1994 turned out to be a colossal event. Various highly regarded Tibetan Buddhist monks attended. At the request of Lama Karma Dorje, the consecration itself was conducted by the Very Venerable Bokar Rinpoche and Khenpo Lodro Dönyo. Attending with them was the young Yangsi Kalu Rinpoche and his parents and attendants. They all had been staying at the KSK Center in Santa Fe where they had given teachings and empowerments in the days preceding the consecration. On the day before the consecration, various members of the KSK sangha, including me, drove the entire entourage on the three-hour drive from Santa Fe to Lorien in procession fashion.

A humorous story arose. Those planning the drive had been incredibly careful and conscientious about how the drive should proceed and which dignitaries should go in which car to appropriately honor their position. Fred Cooper, our KSK President, rented a beautiful Lincoln Continental automobile to lead the procession. Yangsi Kalu Rinpoche, his parents and attendant were to ride in that first car. The second car in the line was mine, a bright red Toyota 4-Runner. V.V. Bokar Rinpoche, Khenpo Dönyo and an attendant were to ride in my car. Virginia Oppenheimer drove the third car in the procession and her car held Lama Dorje and two other monks who were attendants. Several other cars followed these first three. We loaded the passengers into the cars in reverse order. First, Lama Dorje and the attendants got into Virginia's car. Then Bokar Rinpoche and Khenpo Dönyo and an attendant got into my car. Then Yangsi Kalu Rinpoche, his parents and attendant were guided into the first car that would lead the procession. Suddenly as they were getting in the car, Yangsi Kalu Rinpoche refused to enter. In fact, in spite of what appeared to be strong reprimands from his parents, Yangsi Kalu Rinpoche was quite adamant about his request. He wanted to ride in the "bright red car". His protest was so apparent that it bore a definite resemblance to what one might call a "temper tantrum" ... an enlightened one to be sure!! Finally, the matter was resolved. Bokar Rinpoche and Khenpo Dönyo and their attendant got out of the "bright red car" and allowed Yangsi Kalu Rinpoche and his parents and his attendant to get into the red car.

As we drove out of the KSK Center to begin our journey north, the tension in the bright red car was palpable! My knowledge of the Tibetan language was insufficient to understand what was being discussed between the young Kalu and his parents, but my knowledge of young children wanting to get their way was more than sufficient to know that a lively discussion was transpiring! Finally, Rinpoche's mother started laughing. She was sitting in the seat behind the driver's seat. She leaned forward to me and said, "Do you know what he was saying?" I said no, I did not. She said he said "I don't know why my wanting to ride in this bright red car was such a surprise to you. I have been looking at that bright red car in the parking lot for the last several days. You should have known that I wanted to ride in it!" His mother said this was true. He had been talking about the bright red car several times during the week. We all laughed, and the tension lifted. The remainder of our journey to Lorien was happy and fun!

We arrived in Lorien the day before the consecration. We settled the Lamas into their lodgings and gave them a chance to rest. We had also given Yangsi Kalu Rinpoche a "Game Boy", which is a digital, hand-held device that you could play games on. I remember at one point when we went to check on the Lamas to see if they needed anything, several of the attendants were sitting on the floor around Yangsi Kalu Rinpoche exploring the Game Boy and playing games on it. It was wonderful to see the delight on their faces as they conquered this new device!

That evening, the folks in Lorien had planned a delightful cookout for the Lamas and their entourage. Among many other foods, we grilled beef ribs over an outdoor fire. There was great joy at dinner time as everyone loved holding those messy ribs and eating the meat down to the bone. Bokar Rinpoche said it reminded him of being in Tibet and roasting meat over an open fire. Dinner was followed by a wondrous fireworks display. Lorien is located in a great outdoor environment far away from city lights. The exploding fireworks against the deep blue-sky were truly awesome.

The next day was the day of consecration. I was literally dumbfounded by the crowds of people that began to arrive. I never imagined such substantial attendance. There must have been close to 200 people there. The folks in Lorien had worked long and hard to have everything in place to host this consecration. Lama Dorje had given us definite instructions about what we needed to do to properly receive this honorable entourage and any guests who would be attending. One of his admonitions included being sure we had plenty of food to feed everyone. And prepare food we did! I myself had 13 large pans of vegetarian lasagna which I brought to Lorien in the back of my 4-Runner! And all the cooks in Lorien had prepared food in like measure! We were extremely grateful that we had "over-prepared" because there were many more people in attendance than we had anticipated. But there was such an abundance of food that we fed the crowd all they could eat and still had food left over to take to a homeless shelter. Lama Dorje taught us well!

But there was one small glitch. Actually, it was a glitch that turned into a blessing. In anticipation of providing adequate shelter for people and food, we had rented a large tent from a rental company in Albuquerque. Charles Dillon and I had spoken to the tent company several times in the weeks preceding the consecration to make certain that they did not forget to deliver the large tent. Well, as things go sometimes, there was some miscommunication. Instead of delivering one tent, they delivered two! Now if you have ever rented tents from a business 140 miles away to be set up in a rural country setting quite far from any major city, you know that renting such tents is not cheap. Charles and I just looked at each other and agreed that two tents were better than NO tents and so they were set up accordingly. Now the gift of this glitch was that we needed every square inch of BOTH these tents to set up a food buffet and provide seating for the many folks who attended the consecration to protect them from the hot and intense New Mexico sun.

And thanks to the hard work and kind care of many folks, the consecration was a huge success. What a joy it was to see the Lamas sitting inside our beautiful little stupa chanting and saying blessings for its future and ours.

At every stage of the work on the stupa, from the initial planning through the construction and the completion, Lama Dorje was there. He was there to bless the land and locate the exact spot where the stupa should be built. He was there when we laid out the "footprint" of the building. He was there when he said prayers and placed treasures in various places in the stupa. He was there when we mixed concrete in wheelbarrows and hoisted it up to the workers putting the concrete and the blocks into place. He was there when we made the hundreds of tsa-tsa that filled the *bhumpa* (dome) on the stupa and placed prayers in them. In fact, he cast many of the tsa-tsa himself in the small, lean-to type shed behind the hut where he lived in Santa Fe. He was there when there were construction problems to be solved. He was there when we were all so tired we couldn't imagine lifting another concrete block. He was there when we took a lunch break and stretched out after the meal for a few moments of rest before returning to our task. He was there as we rested to give us teachings and answer questions. He was there at the end of each work day as we tidied up the work area and secured the tools and equipment for the next Saturday's work. And he was there in the car for the 3-hour journey back to Santa Fe. Lama never asked anyone to do any work that he himself had not done.

Lama Dorje consecrated the name of this stupa as Kagyu Mila Guru. This name was carefully and skillfully chosen by Lama. Kagyu represented the Kagyu lineage of Tibetan Buddhism. The name Mila was for Milarepa, one of Tibetan Buddhism's most revered saints who was also much beloved by Herman Rednick, the Lorien community's first spiritual teacher and original founder. Students of Herman's in this community were also familiar with this Tibetan teacher. Guru was chosen because of the community's devotion to their teacher Herman Rednick. Lama also chose this name because when spoken "Mila Guru" sounds very similar to the Spanish word "Milagro" which means "*miracle.*" Thus, the name also recognizes the long-established, Spanish community in northern New Mexico where this stupa was built. Lama always respects and honors any community where stupas are built and naming this stupa with both an English and a Spanish meaning was a very skillful way to accomplish this.

Here is what Charles Dillon, the general contractor for the stupa, has to say about Lama Karma Dorje:

I am so grateful to Lama Karma Dorje for all the experiences he has led us through since we met him. He knew from the beginning what could happen here ... stepping out with us on the brink of the building ... the shape it takes ... and of its unforeseen beauty. He led us from the teachings of Herman Rednick into the Tibetan Buddhist path. I thank you. We all thank you because you have guided us so carefully.

Lama Dorje has done so much for us ... even when he was not physically here. Lama and all the other beings who assist him have brought incredible beauty to our lives. He has been the one above all others that continues to bring these things into form ... to bring spirit into form. I am so thankful to him. It makes me weep when I think of him.

Here is how another person described the experience of working on the building of this stupa with Lama Dorje:

All I can say is that people who don't put their backs into building a sacred structure, wear out their shoes, stress out their checkbooks really don't know what they are missing. What a gift Lama Dorje gave us ... the opportunity to work on not just one stupa, but two! There is a certain kind of freedom you get from working hard for no personal gain. In working to build these stupas, I know these moments of freedom. But Lama Dorje has spent his whole life full of this kind of work. How free, I think, he must feel! What a gift working on a stupa brings!

- *Anna R.*

Many students recall seemingly "magical" moments that occurred while building the stupa.

It was fall, close to winter and getting cold. The land the stupa sits on is almost 8,400 feet in elevation. We were all set to pour the concrete slab but there was a forecast for snow. When Lama arrived, we asked him about this concern. He simply smiled and said we should go ahead and pour the slab. We did, and it started to snow. It snowed around all four sides of the slab and on back out to the mountains and the mesa, but not a drop of snow fell on the beautifully smooth concrete slab floor.

- *Hilece R.*

As I look at this wondrous stupa today, I marvel at its great beauty. On a personal level, it will always serve for me as a reminder of my mother. But its true meaning is much broader. Since its consecration, it has been blessed and prayed for by many visiting Tibetan lamas, learned teachers and serious practitioners. It sits in its radiant glory at the foot of the Sangre de Cristo mountains with views of unparalleled splendor in each and every direction. Just viewing the stupa is a gift to one's eyes and one's heart. But as I and others who worked on the building of this stupa have remarked, as beautiful as this glorious structure is, nothing can surmount the joy and the heartfelt goodness that we experienced building and bringing this stupa into form, working side by side, concrete block by concrete block with the great and glorious being that is Lama Karma Dorje.

KAGYU MILA GURU WORK CREW

LAMA DORJE, MASTER BUILDER, READY FOR WORK

CHARLES DILLON, GENERAL CONTRACTOR, SURVEYS THE WORK

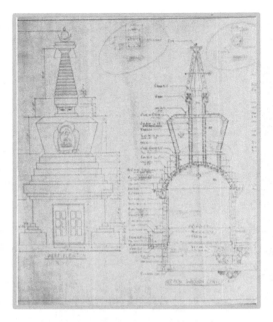

THE KMG BUILDING PLAN

LAMA DORJE SAYS PRAYERS TO BLESS THE LAND WHERE THE STUPA WILL SIT

LAMA DORJE AND CHARLES COUNTING CONCRETE BLOCKS

LAYING OUT THE FOUNDATION LINES FOR THE STUPA

FORMING THE CONCRETE DOME

**FORMING THE BHUMPA WITH
ADOBE BLOCKS AND CONCRETE**

**LAMA DORJE AND OTHERS WORK
ON SHAPING THE BHUMPA**

**LAMA DORJE MIXING CONCRETE
IN A WHEELBARROW**

**LAMA DORJE PAINTING MANTRAS
ON THE INSIDE OF THE BHUMPA**

**LAMA DORJE MAKES CERTAIN
THE PETALS ARE CORRECT**

PLACING THE PETALS

POURING TSA-TSA'S

KAGYU MILA GURU STUPA

YANGSI KALU RINPOCHE AND H.H. BOKAR
RINPOCHE CONSECRATING THE STUPA

THE ALTAR INSIDE THE KMG STUPA

THE STUPA SITS AT THE BASE
OF THE SANGRE DE CRISTO
MOUNTAINS

CROWN ON THE KMG STUPA BUILT BY BYRON
WICKSTROM STUDENT OF LAMA DORJE

KAGYU MILA GURU STUPA AT SUNSET

KYANG TSIK CHORTEN
THE RACICOT STUPA

QUESTA, NEW MEXICO

KYANG TSIK CHORTEN

Just as Lama Dorje embraces "all creatures great and small", so too does he manifest stupas. And the story of this stupa is special. This stupa was built by Steve and Anna Racicot, long-time students of Herman Rednick who became students of Lama Karma Dorje and Tibetan Buddhism. Steve and Anna were part of the core group that built the Kagyu Mila Guru stupa in Questa. Along with others, they worked faithfully and vigorously for three years bringing that stupa into the beautiful form that it is today. And the genesis of this stupa, Kyang Tsik Chorten, is especially sweet. Anna describes it as follows:

> *Work on the Kagyu Mila Guru stupa was finishing up and Lama Dorje was walking beside me up the path from the cement mixer to the stupa. I was glad that it was nearly finished because it was beautiful to bring it to completion. But the glorious process of building it was nearing an end. I said nothing. Lama said something like, "Do you think you and Steve (my husband) could build a little stupa on your land?" He said it would not be a big one and it would not have a bhumpa (the rounded, bowl like shape near the top). It would be a Khang Tsik Chorten. He said it would still be a real stupa, called a chorten in Tibetan, which meant "having dharma." I remember thinking that even building a small stupa would be a difficult undertaking but one I would love to do. Steve felt the same way and that fall we put in the foundation for such a stupa and all that goes with that.*

Kyang Tsik stupa sits on a piece of land with striking views in all directions. To the north is the majestic San Juan range at the southern end of the Rocky Mountains. The lofty peaks of Mount Blanca overlook its reach. To the west lies the open range encircling the stately peaks of San Antonio and Ute mountains. To the south stands the sacred Taos Mountain. The stupa itself lies nestled in the Sangre de Cristo mountains to the East.

Steve and Anna Racicot who built this stupa, describe it as follows:

We naturally thought that a Tibetan Buddhist stupa, in addition to being filled with "tsa-tsa", which themselves are miniature stupas, would house statues of Tibetan Buddhist deities, particularly our favorites, Chenrezig, Tara , the Buddha and our beloved saint, Milarepa. We knew from the time we closed the bumpa on the Kagyu Mila Guru stupa, that we needed to also include a representation of our local deity, our Lady of Guadalupe. Nevertheless, we were surprised, and I must say delighted, when Lama Dorje told us to put into our little stupa whatever we were devoted to, and we were devoted to a lot ... a real smorgasbord of holy beings ... a real pantheon. Now we could include our devotion to Christ, Mary, the angels, the archangels and Steve's longtime devotion to Kali. A friend who was immersed in Hinduism was traveling to India. We asked her to please bring us a statue of Kali and she did. We realized we had something, at least in the form of texts, from all of the world's religions except Islam. We could not leave Islam out. We had another friend on the Sufi path who gave us a cloth print of the first words of the Koran. The teachings of our root guru, Herman Rednick, were well represented. They included a postcard of one of his paintings of Christ.

When we visited Lama Dorje in Santa Fe, he asked what we had included inside the stupa. *"What about your ancestors?"* he asked. We told him our ancestors are from England, France and Germany. He shook his head and said, *"No. No. No."* He wanted the ancestors of the land on which we were building the stupa to be remembered. Again, we were delighted. We have always loved and admired the people who lived in this beautiful, but often harsh, environment.

As fate would have it, as we were clearing the spot on which we intended to build the stupa, Steve found a very unusual point or arrowhead. The small body of it was curved and excellently made, but since it was curved, it would never have penetrated nor flown correctly. We mentioned this to Lama Yeshe and Lama Tsering who were painting mantras on the inside of the KMG stupa. Yeshe took it to a friend of his at Taos Pueblo. This man was also puzzled by it but determined it must have been created for a ceremonial purpose. With Lama Dorje's approval we included this point and other similar objects in the stupa.

Lama Dorje challenged us with the idea of building a stupa on our property. He delighted us with the suggestion to be inclusive with the objects we placed in the stupa. Now we find ourselves delighted when we go to walk, approach the stupa with prayers in our minds and make small offerings.

As Westerners, we were initially more attracted to stupas into which a person could enter. Now that we have a little stupa around which a person can circumambulate, we understand the true beauty of this form. As we walk through this world, how delightful it is to walk around this stupa, this thing of beauty which sings its spiritual song into the morning. Thank you, Lama Dorje.

PREPARING THE SCAFFOLDING AND
FORMS FOR THE STUPA STEPS

THE STUPA WAITING FOR
ITS FINISHING COAT OF STUCCO

ANNA PREPARES THE TSOG SHING
FOR PLACEMENT IN THE
CENTER OF THE STUPA

STEVE PREPARES THE STUPA
FOR THE NEXT PHASE OF CONSTRUCTION

LAMA DORJE
SECRET YOGI

LAMA KARMA DORJE
Secret Yogi

Lama Dorje lives a simple, transparent life. He lives in a small, single room in the main house of the Kagyu Shenpen Kunchab Tibetan Buddhist Center on Airport Road in Santa Fe, New Mexico. He has lived in that room for over 25 years. Before that he lived in a small building at the Center that could most accurately be described as a "hut." His wants are minimal and his needs only a slight bit greater. His activities over the almost 45 years that he has lived there are centered around prayer and meditation and leading and advising the many people who come to the Center to pursue a spiritual life.

In addition, as the leader of the Center he is also its Chief Operating Officer. He is responsible for all the myriad decisions required of any businessperson running an institution in today's business world. He must continually determine and decide the course of action for many administrative and management situations that arise in the running of a non-profit religious center. As one who has observed him over many years, I can tell you without hesitation that he is a brilliant businessman and an awesome problem solver. He doesn't merely sit on his seat and propound what needs to be done, he jumps right into the fray and contributes whatever is required, be it brains or be it brawn. I have literally seen him creatively solve and implement architectural building problems not even imagined or considered by onsite building professionals. At the same time, I have seen him physically cleaning out an overloaded septic system by literally shoveling out its contents. Lama Dorje's commitment to building and maintaining an active and vital Tibetan Buddhist Center is so absolute and comprehensive that many people who have come to visit the Center have, at times, thought of him as merely the Center's caretaker.

But apart from being a masterful teacher, an incredible builder and a superb businessman, Lama is also an enlightened and secret yogi. Now what does this mean? Most people possess some kind of skill, whether fully developed or totally neglected. And some people even possess extraordinary skills. Think of a painter whose work you know and admire. For example, think of Norman Rockwell. His paintings have hung on many great and unusual walls and have appeared on the magazine covers of publications in wide circulation. I think we can fairly say that he has extraordinary painting skills. I myself am a painter. My paintings have hung on only a few walls and have never been reproduced on any magazine covers. I am a painter of ordinary skill. Norman Rockwell is a painter with extraordinary skill. Or how about the field of music? Andrea Bocelli's voice has warmed the hearts of many, whether he is singing an operatic masterpiece or a contemporary chant. It is practically inarguable that his voice is extraordinary. You or I attempting such vocal endeavors are surely relegated to the privacy of our own shower stalls! At best, our musical talent is quite ordinary. These types of examples, persons possessing extraordinary skills versus those of us with ordinary skills, appear in many walks of life among many people. In the world of tangible skills, it becomes relatively easy to understand and accept that people with extraordinary skills do exist.

In the world of less tangible skills, skills that we cannot ordinarily feel, see or touch, we are often skeptical of those claiming extraordinary skills. And rightly so. Admittedly, our world is full of charlatans claiming many diverse "extraordinary" skills. I am a lawyer. I was trained in hard evidence and tangible proof. These skills are very necessary in today's world where information abounds with equal, apparent credibility alongside misinformation. We must each read, feel and decide for ourselves what we believe and what we reject.

Watching Lama Dorje is an exercise in humility. He never tries to be the center of attention nor does he assign to himself extraordinary qualities. People who have observed Lama Dorje do or say something unusual will sometimes say to him, "Oh, Lama, you are psychic." Lama just laughs and responds, *"I no psychic."* Here is an experience that one student shared:

> *We have all had the feeling that there is more to someone than meets the eye. Lama is one of those for whom we might say that what we see in our interactions with him is a small fraction of who he really is.*
> *Our son, Joe, when he was in the second or third grade, must have sensed this. Joe came up with a science project to see if people could influence objects with their minds. He asked his subjects to roll three dice while not trying to roll any particular number as a control and then to try*

to roll a six on each die. His hypothesis was that when people tried to roll a certain number, they sometimes succeeded more than the average would otherwise.

Joe recalled a visit we had with Lama Dorje in Santa Fe when he asked Lama to participate in this experiment. At first, Lama told him that he did not want to participate, but when Joe explained that it was an important project for his schoolwork, Lama agreed. Lama quickly rolled the dice the required number of times and when Joe asked him to roll sixes, Lama rolled all sixes five times in a row. "The really crazy thing" Joe recalled, "is that he was able to do it every time. And he was the only person ever to do this."

There are stories in all traditions of the hidden holy man or woman. Their humility is so deep and so genuine that most people regard them as relatively unimportant. Meanwhile, these people may be real saints or accomplished yogis. Lama Dorje is, for me, one of those rare and wonderful people.

- Anna R.

From time to time, students of Lama Dorje and others are given a glimpse into the hidden yogi that is Lama Dorje.

On Saturdays for many months, Lama Dorje went from Santa Fe to Lorien to work on the construction of the stupa there. I participated in those workdays. On this particular day, the workers were constructing the steps representing the four immeasurables. From there, at a height of probably 12- 15 feet, a bucket of cement was accidentally dropped on my head. I instantly hit the ground. Lama came running over to me and in that moment, I saw him clearly as the personification of the Buddha.

-Rachel S.

And,

One Wednesday evening, at the end of Chenrezig practice, I witnessed an unusual happening. As Virginia was collecting the texts for the practice, both I and the person sitting next to me distinctly saw Lama visually emerge from his seat as an enormous manifestation of Chenrezig. I could not explain it except to say I am certain of what I saw!

- Rachel S.

David Bates, a longtime and devoted student of Lama Dorje, relates an event that happened the first time David met Lama Dorje. He had driven out to Tres Orejas to meet Lama and after working on the front porch of the gompa with Lama and Norbert, David and Lama sat down on the front porch, looking out over the Taos Valley. Here is what happened:

> *That day, after we had finished working on the gompa, I was sitting on the porch with Lama. We were sitting there talking and looking out over the beautiful Taos valley. Lama said, "Oh look! There are deer running past." And I saw them. Then they passed and a couple of hunters came up and asked, "Which way did the deer go?" Lama pointed in the opposite direction. And then I thought, "What was that?" Although I thought I saw them, there were really no deer there at all. And then Lama had sort of lied to the hunters by pointing in the wrong direction. But in truth, there had been no real deer there; there were no real hunters either, even though I thought I saw them. So I left there a little confused and trying to think what this teaching might have meant.*

David said he believed that Lama Dorje had somehow manifested this event to either teach David a lesson or to demonstrate for him Lama's extraordinary abilities.

It is never easy to accept or understand those events that defy our normal everyday perception. It is easy to dismiss them by calling them "figments of imagination" or questioning the sanity of the person who experiences such events. Yet, these seemingly inexplicable situations happen. I leave it to you, the reader, to decide and employ for yourself their credibility.

But before dismissing these testimonies as not credible, it is worthwhile to consider the perceptions of others. A longtime student of Lama Dorje's says the following:

> *Lama is truly an enlightened being. His teachings are profound and even devastating for someone like me who tends to rely on my own selfish tendencies in this life! I cannot think of anyone who has shown more kindness ... not kindness in the western sense, but true kindness in the sense of moving one along the path to enlightenment. Lama teaches at a deep level the meaning and fundamental path of Buddhism. Lama's mirror-like mind continues to shine and reveal the truth, disturbing the*

166

illusory nature of our actions. For this, I am thankful. Deep vows and prayers for his longevity.

- *Paul S.*

In the material included in this section, I am not asking that you accept or reject anything. I am merely the recorder, the messenger if you will. But what I do want to bring to you are accounts from people who have observed or received the blessing of Lama Dorje's extraordinary qualities, qualities that often seem prophetic. If you ask him about these qualities, he will quickly say, *"I no psychic."* Maybe he is or maybe he is not. I cannot answer that. But what I know is that Lama Dorje is able to tap into knowledge and information that is not available to ordinary minds like my own. If you remain skeptical, that is your choice. But even a short search will reveal that history is replete with individuals who have had these extraordinary abilities. I invite you to read the stories contained in this section and decide for yourself what you believe and what you relegate to the category of "unbelievable." But the people who have written these accounts of their experiences with Lama Dorje are not folks caught up in the world of "magical thinking." They are all people with a high degree of worldly sophistication and intelligence. They are smart, independent thinkers. Their stories merely record their own individual experiences without judgment or bias. May these stories present their own wisdom and perspective.

A PAPER CLIP

-   Alice Herter

I am a lawyer. I am also a born skeptic. Things like "faith" and "trust" are not feelings that came naturally to me. In my world, faith and trust were attributes to be earned. Additionally, as a lawyer, I was trained to "follow the facts." Speculation and conjecture had little traction in my view of the world. *"Show me the proof"* formed my base of operation. With this as background, I share the following story of Lama Karma Dorje.

As my career as a lawyer progressed, one of the career goals that I had for myself was that I wanted to become a judge. After I had been practicing law for over twenty years, a position for a judgeship came open. At that time, I had experience as a lawyer both in private practice and in the government sector. In government, I had experience at both the federal and state government levels. Also, I was known to the legal community and had indications of support from individuals within the legal profession as well as political support. In keeping with the requirements for consideration for this judgeship, I completed all the necessary application work for the position including letters of reference on my behalf.

After submitting my application, I spoke to Lama Dorje about what I was doing. He said, "Oh no. You no become a judge." I was surprised by his reaction and asked why he said that. He said, "When you are a judge, you have the power to send people to prison. You send someone to prison and they come and shoot you." I could not deny that this could happen but I considered it highly unlikely. Nonetheless, I knew Lama Dorje never said things carelessly or without legitimate cause. So based on his advice, I withdrew my application.

Subsequently, a judge was named to fill this position. He was a good lawyer and an excellent choice. However, about one year after his appointment, a man who had been sentenced to prison came to the courthouse and shot this judge dead. It was a terrible tragedy and a shock to the community. It was especially shocking to me because of the warning that Lama Dorje had given me a year or so before when I wanted to apply for that judgeship myself.

But the story does not end there.

About a year later, I was asked to become the Executive Director of the state's public employee pension system. This was a big decision for me. I had served as General Counsel to this organization and had an understanding of what would be required. I also knew that it was a political job that added an overlay to the organization's operation. I discussed the job offer with Lama Dorje. Lama said that I should take that job if I wanted it. But, he issued a strong warning. He said, "If you take this job, you must not ever take anything home from the office ... not even a paper clip." I was surprised by this warning. I am not a thief, and I knew that Lama Dorje knew this. But I have seldom known anyone who worked anywhere ... be it in the private sector or the public sector ... who did not at some time take some small item home from their office either consciously or inadvertently. For example, it would not be uncommon for someone to take work home from the office with a writing pen or pencil tucked in their pocket or purse. But I knew Lama well enough at that point that I knew he didn't make statements like this lightly or in jest. He meant exactly what he said: "Do not take anything home from your office ... not even a paper clip." The warning was quite clear.

And so I took the job, ever mindful of Lama Dorje's warning. And because of that warning, I exercised great care and caution in all my dealings with the agency. For example, in my job as Executive Director, I was required to have three phones ... a desk phone, a car phone and a cell phone. From the beginning of my tenure, I asked our Comptroller to provide me each month with a listing of all the calls I made from these phones along with the length of time of the call and the cost. At that time, the state had what was called a "WATTS" system that automatically recorded this information for all calls made from any phone within the agency. Each month I went through this listing and highlighted with a yellow marker all calls on the listing that were personal for me ... for example, calls that I might have made to my doctor's office to cancel or reschedule an appointment or something like that. As an aside, I might add that I did not make many personal calls from my office because I rarely had the time for personal matters at work. Nonetheless, I went through the many pages of recorded calls that I had made for the month, highlighted the ones that were personal, and then added the cost of the call as stated on the document. I then wrote a personal check for the total amount of these calls and returned this information along with my check to the Comptroller.

Another example of exercising care and caution was photocopying documents. I had access to many photocopiers in my office. It would have been quick and easy to simply make a copy of a personal document I needed on one of these agency copiers with little real time or expense to the agency. Nonetheless, I did not do that. When I needed a copy of a document for personal purposes, I went to Kinko's, a commercial copy center, and made the copy or copies there. I cite these examples to indicate the diligence with which I followed Lama Dorje's advice. I did not take even so much as a paper clip for my personal use.

I held the position of Executive Director of the state's pension system for about 6 years. I was, in fact, the retirement system's first female Director. During that time, speaking modestly and somewhat to my credit, the agency experienced great success. The size of the pension fund increased from about 1.5 billion dollars to 8.6 billion dollars. That was a substantial increase over a six-year period. Also, for the first time in the pension fund's history, the fund was "fully funded." We also were able to get an Amendment to the state's Constitution passed by the public in a statewide general election that provided constitutional protections for the pension fund and its recipients. Prior to the passage of this Constitutional Amendment, the state's pension fund was a creature of state statute that could be changed by legislative whim. Further, the Amendment also provided that the pension system was to be managed solely for the benefit of the pension fund itself and its recipients and participants. As a practical matter this meant that in utilizing and investing the pension system funds, the standard to be applied was to be solely to benefit the fund and by contrast, could not be used to benefit some political purpose or individual plan of a state legislator or public official.

It will probably come as no surprise, but politics and money have a great attraction. As the pension fund increased, so too did the interest of politicians in trying to claim usage of these funds for non-pension purposes. Considerable pressure was applied on me by various high-level state officials to influence the use of the pension fund monies. I resisted this pressure because my purpose and loyalty were to the recipients and participants of the pension system and not to the politicians. It will probably also come as no surprise, that certain high-level officials, namely the State Auditor, the State Treasurer, and the Majority Leader of the State Senate, came after me. They announced publicly and in state-

171

wide media and newspapers, that they were launching an investigation into my conduct because they alleged that I had misused government property. They set up a team of auditors and investigators to scrutinize all the agency records to prove their erroneous claims. The investigation covered three years of my tenure in office. At the conclusion of their investigation, the only thing they found over this three-year period was $14.96 worth of telephone calls that they claimed were my personal calls. Even this claim was unfounded. They claimed that these calls were personal because they were calls made to non-commercial phone numbers. This was true but these phone numbers were the home phone numbers of various pension fund Board Members who, on occasion, I had to call at their home or private numbers.

*In the end, the investigators could not find even a "**paper clip**" that I had taken. Lama Dorje's dire warning when I decided to take the job was well-founded. How did he know what my future looked like? How did he know to caution me so strongly? I would like to think that even without his warning I would not have taken anything of real value from the agency, but his warning caused me to be ever-vigilant right from the start of my tenure. His warning caused me to constantly monitor and document the record about my use or non-use of government property.*

Being falsely accused is difficult to endure. This is especially true when the false claims are broadcast in newspapers, on television and other public media. It is quite easy to want to "get even" and seek revenge. It is quite easy to want to launch a counter-offensive. But here again, Lama Dorje cautioned me against doing this. He said, *"You no get angry ... you no try to get even. Karma will take care of this. These people, these false accusers may seem to be winning, but they cannot escape karma."* So, I held my tongue and corralled my vengeful instincts. I believe in karma. I believe we reap what we sow. And believing that made me embrace Lama Dorje's advice.

About a year after I left my position as Executive Director of the pension fund, the State Auditor, the State Treasurer and the Senate Majority Leader (my false accusers) were indicted by the federal government on racketeering and bribery charges and received prison sentences as a consequence. Not only had Lama Karma Dorje seen my future when I took this job but he also knew what would happen to my false accusers.

172

LAMA, THE BRIDGE-BUILDER

- *Gabrielle Herbertson*

I met Lama Dorje during a dark time for my mind. It was seven years after my guru, Herman Rednick, had died, myself in the bardo of knowing he was not gone, but without enough facility or faith to experience it. Herman had told us that if we continued beyond his death to walk the path he had taught — the path of love, compassion, and service — in some number of years, we would meet other teachers who would show us the secrets of the universe. I believe now that Lama Karma Dorje was the fulfillment of that prediction.

This lama, with utter purity and secret omniscience, may have been the only one of his tradition arriving in the West who could have made the bridge for us between Herman's Christ-guru in my heart and Buddha and his spiritual brothers of Tibetan Buddhism. Lama recognized Herman as an authentic teacher. "*You must keep your samaya [vows] with him,*" he said. "*And also, if you want to learn the methods of Buddhism, I will be happy to teach you. Then you will have two wings.*"So, we began to learn of the Lord of Compassion, Chenrezig, Lama's heart practice, and of Milarepa, whose image Herman had painted many times from his own inner vision, because he felt so close to that great yogi.

In our lingering heartbreak at losing our beloved guide Herman in physical form, we had kept his house exactly as he had left it, as if time had stopped. We did not know how to go on. Lama told us, with great tenderness, that we could choose some special things of Herman's to include in a shrine for him in a place of honor in one room, and then we could move again, open up the painting studio, make his house into the welcoming contemplative space Herman had hoped it would become.

Lama also said, "*In my country, we honor the parinirvana, the day of passing of our teachers, and the students come together and pray to him and receive his blessings on that day.*" Thus, we began the tradition of our Herman Memorial around April 17th of each year. "*Cook great amounts of food for everyone,*" Lama said. "*Generosity.*" Lama himself came to lead the first memorial.

And then Lama Dorje built our stupa, at Alice's request, in the Kagyu tradition. He named it Kagyu Mila Guru Stupa, for Milarepa, for the guru, and because "Mila Guru" sounded like "Milagro"--*miracle* in Spanish. This would invite our Hispanic neighbors to be at ease. It is Buddha's mind; it is Herman's memory. He called it a peace monument.

We listened as Lama taught us. He said the stupa was the guru's mind. The temple, where we meet to share Herman's teachings, was the guru's speech. Herman's house was the guru's body. And in that body, we came together each Saturday with Lama, for a potluck lunch (with Alice's lasagna!) after working all morning with Lama. Our families and children also came and made the stupa with Lama, mixing cement, carrying buckets, stacking cinderblocks. Dusty, tired, and utterly joyous, we ate, and then sat in the shrine room while Lama spoke to us. Precious words, stories, treasures that would open even further, later, in our minds.

And so it was that Lama Karma Dorje--with the compassion of a mother for her little children, and a skill that astounds me the more I recall it, brought together a sincere and seeking little collection of aspirants with connections to both Lord Christ and Lord Buddha, from one country to an adjoining one, without even noticing a border.

BRINGING RAIN
- *Debra Snyderman*

Debra Snyderman, a student of Lama Dorje's, who has lived near the stupa for many years and witnessed its many changes, relates the following story about Lama.

Somewhere around 1983, Lama Dorje was invited on a trip to Ecuador with one of his Los Angeles students, Juan Nigari. Juan was visiting Lama Dorje in Santa Fe when Kalu Rinpoche was there. Juan asked Rinpoche if he could take Lama o a trip to Ecuador and Peru. Rinpoche gave his permission for the trip.

In Quito, Lama met and befriended Father Davila, a Catholic priest. They became good friends. Father Davila made arrangements to take Lama Dorje around Ecuador and show him some of the country. About 40 miles outside of Quito was the village of Rafal where Lama's student Juan's wife had family. It was a very special family. The parents had a large piece of land. They had 2 wonderful daughters and 5 successful sons: a surgeon, a doctor, an engineer, a lawyer and a police officer. The sons each had a home on this land surrounded by adobe walls. Lama and Juan stayed there as guests. An Indian man and his family also lived there and worked there as servants.

For 6 months, much of Ecuador had been in a severe drought. Crops were failing and there was much suffering. Juan told the Indian man that Lama Dorje could make it rain. Juan had heard this from Peggy and Michael from Taos, (Tres Orejas) New Mexico, who had witnessed Lama do this during a time of great need. The Indian man went to Lama and said, "Please, please, make it rain. My people are struggling to grow food." Lama said to Juan, "Why did you tell him that?" Lama felt very nervous about the request and was worried about failure and embarrassment and couldn't sleep.

Father Davila came to take Lama and Juan on a trip in his new car, made in Korea. They visited an Indian village where corn grew tall and strong. The people there had many cows and used the dung to grow corn. It was a beautiful place near a big lake formed by a dam. Lama said the mountains looked torma (offerings)! Lama found a quiet place to pray in the village and got permission to do a fire puja (ceremony). As the fire was still burning, raindrops suddenly began to fall. Juan called out, "Lama! Lama! Rain coming! Rain coming!" Ever humble, Lama said it was a "light rain" but it was "better than nothing."

That night, on the way back to Rafal, clouds gathered and it began to rain. This was not a light rain. In fact, it rained and rained and rained so hard that parts of the road were washed away. Father Davila's car was not a 4-wheel drive and they had to stop and wait in places for people to show up and fix the road.

The villagers in Rafal were deeply grateful to Lama Dorje. For his remaining days there, the villagers came each day with wonderful offerings of oranges, bananas and delicious tamales. Father Davila also gave Lama Dorje a beautiful glass cross, which hangs to this day on Lama's wall.

STOPPING RAIN
- *Hilece Rose*

Lama Dorje married my husband Michael and me here in Lorien at the Herman Rednick temple. Starting about ten days before the wedding, it poured rain every single day, not just afternoon showers but showers each day all day, a somewhat unusual circumstance here in northern New Mexico. We were especially concerned because we had planned an outside reception after the wedding under tents. We called Lama, telling him our concern and worry about the rain for the wedding. He told us two things: first, he said not to worry, and second, he told us rain is a blessing. So, we relaxed.

The morning of the wedding, the rain poured down in torrents. My mom, my sister, my husband and me were in the house getting ready. When Lama came up the driveway, the rain suddenly stopped and the sun came out shining brilliantly. In fact, the path we walked to the temple was so dry that we did not even get our shoes or our clothes wet! But the moment the wedding and the reception were over and Lama Dorje was leaving, the heavens opened with a torrential downpour!

TRIBUTE FROM FRED COOPER
President, KSK Tibetan Buddhist Center
Santa Fe, New Mexico

LAMA KARMA DORJE

A Hidden Bodhisattva

I met Lama Dorje in 1982 after taking refuge with Guru Vajradhara Tai Situ Rinpoche while he was visiting Project Tibet in Santa Fe. Tai Situ was part of the group that escaped from Tibet along with Paljor Thondrup, who owned Project Tibet. Two weeks later, HE Kalu Rinpoche came to Santa Fe and gave a large number of empowerments and teachings at KSK Buddhist Center at Ken and Sally Maynard's housed on Irvine Street as well as other venues. I met Lama Dorje at that time. Lama Dorje had arrived in Santa Fe in 1981. During his 1982 trip to Santa Fe, Kalu Rinpoche requested Lama Dorje and his students to begin construction of the KSK stupa. When my wife, Cathy and I were going to India in 1985, having been invited to give talks at a Physics conference in Bhubaneshwar, Lama Dorje gave me photographs of the then-current state of the stupa project to show to Kalu Rinpoche. This enabled me to spend quite a lot of personal time with Kalu Rinpoche. This was an incredible act of generosity.

Starting about 1983, I became active at the center participating in the Chenrezig and Green Tara pujas as well as sitting meditations. At that time, Sarah Harding was serving as translator as well as giving classes on how to do the various pujas. My entire family participated in the construction of the KSK stupa. My two children, Lottie and David, helped Chagdud Tulku with the making of the Buddha statue. In 1989 I went to Brown University to teach for a year and started a small branch of KSK there. While I was at Brown, Kalu Rinpoche requested that I become President of KSK, and I have been honored with that responsibility ever since. Lama Dorje has continuously defended that decision against people who were not happy with my being President. Lama Dorje has also supported my inviting various teachers to give extended teachings and empowerments at KSK.

I have had the good fortune of knowing Lama Dorje for forty years now and can witness the love and devotion he has inspired in all that come in contact with him. When my father-in-law came to Santa Fe, he met Lama Dorje and made an offering to him, telling me that he had finally met an honest religious leader. This was quite something since he was a tremendous skeptic, especially of the religious teachers he had met in the Catholic faith.

It is quite difficult to fathom someone like Lama Dorje. Outwardly he lives the life of a simple monk. Most of his outer religious life is seen in his leading pujas and spending the rest of his time, when he is not counseling people, doing prayers and meditation in his room. He does not do much formal teaching, which is one of the reasons I started giving teachings that I had received from Guru Vajrdhara Tai Situ Rinpoche and H.E. Mingyur Rinpoche on a regular basis. Starting about 15 years ago, I received the transmission of Mahamudra from these two gurus. Lama Dorje's encouragement to do this teaching has led to a great deepening of my understanding of the dharma.

By observing Lama Dorje's actions in dealing with all types of situations, one can clearly see that he is a true Bodhisattva. He has truly perfected the six parameters:

1. Generosity: He is available to see anyone at any time to give help and advice. Having tea with Lama Dorje is the way he freely offers his time and knowledge. He is also totally unattached to money. His motto is "Money in. Money out" ... with no sticky fingers. Every time the Center was in need of funds, he would miraculously pull out an envelope of donations he had received and hand me all the money necessary for the project, whether it was for repairs or for the purchase of Shenpen Ling [the apartment building adjacent to the Center that we purchased to generate additional income for the Center.] He gave the money without any hesitation. This is different from my thoughts at the same time when I stopped to consider how much I could afford to give the Center without having any reservations. His attitude is the true paramita of generosity.

2. Virtue (Morality): Lama lives the life of a simple monk and observes all the precepts. He is quick to point out areas of your life where there is any gray area in your actions and behavior.

3. Patience: Lama Dorje shows infinite patience in dealing with all the people who come to see him ... some with some pretty crazy behavior! He treats everyone with respect and does his best to help them. He has also had to deal with a hematoma of the brain following a car accident and partial

paralysis as a result of a stroke. Even so, he continues all his duties without making a big deal about any of his quite significant physical issues.

4. <u>Diligence</u>: Lama Dorje has accomplished the completion of several stupas, the starting of three Buddhists Centers and he continues oversight of both Santa Fe and Taos sanghas. He also remains extremely diligent with his practice. When he is not otherwise occupied, he is in his room doing meditation practice.

5. <u>Meditation</u>: Lama Dorje has perfected meditation. This is apparent when you meditate with him or when you are just having tea with him. The fact that all his channels and winds have been perfected leads you to automatically go into a meditative state of calmness and clarity when you are in his presence.

6. <u>Wisdom</u>: Lama Dorje has clearly perfected the Wisdom paramita. This has led to powers of clairvoyance which he displays at different times when appropriate.

Lama Dorje does not give many formal teachings, apart from explaining how to do pujas and other rituals. For me, he gives his teachings while we are drinking tea together. As I tell him what I am doing or planning to do, he will say something to me that shocks me. It may or may not have anything to do with what we are talking about. It always refers to something going on in my life where I am displaying pride, attachment, or jealousy, usually on a subtle level that is hidden from me. When he comes out with these statements, they at first shock me, almost make me angry, but then they help me confront those areas where I need to do more work on my ego attachment. He might make a statement which points out that my generosity in teaching dharma is obscured somewhat by having pride that I am a teacher of Buddhism. We are not usually talking about these issues directly when he comes out with these statements. He has the *siddhi* (great wisdom and understanding) of knowing what obscurations exist in the person he is with and then … he just points it out! Sometimes this seems brutal, but it is quite an effective method. The words he uses are not always straightforward. He might say, "you know you are not a Lama … yet you are teaching." Well, that is true, but he is pointing out something else here. As a result of being a Bodhisattva and having this wonderful siddhi, he is loved and adored by all his students.

In summary, it has been both my pleasure and my privilege to know and work with Lama Karma Dorje as the President of the KSK Center. He has led this Center with clarity and direction through hard and lean times with the goodness and simplicity that reflects both who Lama is and what Buddhism endeavors to manifest.

EPILOGUE

EPILOGUE

Archbishop Desmond Tutu is quoted as saying, *"Do your little bit of good where you are. It's those little bits of good put together that overwhelm the world."* I think that is what many of us try to do. We go to work. We take care of children and our households. We pay the utility bills. We go to our various places of worship. And we engage in some social activities for fun and entertainment. As we do these things, and even in between these things, we try to *"do a little bit of good."* These efforts are not to be minimized. Balancing all of our obligations with doing our *little bit of good* takes commitment and energy. But what about those who forgo many of these worldly pursuits to focus more fully on doing good? What can we say about their sacrifice to do more than just *a little bit of good*?

Starting as a young man, Lama Karma Dorje has devoted his life to doing good. He was the oldest son of a Tibetan family living in Sikkim. While not rich, the family owned land making them far wealthier than many of their neighbors and local residents. As the oldest son and according to cultural tradition, Lama Dorje could have claimed and controlled these resources as his own. Instead, at an early age he entered the monastery and began religious studies. He continued his training in the monastery up through completing his three-year retreat and taking 253 monk vows. After retreat, he returned to the house his 88-year-old lama had left him high in the Himalayan mountains. Here he intended to live the simple and quiet life of a Tibetan Buddhist monk. But this solitary and contemplative life was not to be. Lama was asked by the head of his lineage, the 16th Gyalwa Karmapa and by his teacher Venerable Kalu Rinpoche to leave his life of quiet simplicity and go to the West to help guide the fledgling Buddhist centers being established there.

Lama Dorje answered that call. Lama left the quiet and contemplative life he had trained for and without even knowing the language of the country where he was being assigned, he came to the big and bustling city of Los Angeles. His knowledge of Western culture was so limited that he was told and believed that he could not even buy rice here, a food that was the main staple of his diet.

But from that challenging beginning, over the next forty-three years, this humble and dedicated lama created and established vital and thriving Tibetan Buddhist Centers, where he initiated and built four beautiful and magnificent stupas. In addition, he constructed and converted dilapidated old adobe buildings into habitable housing, he built mediation buildings, retreat rooms, housing for precious Buddhist texts, and other ancillary structures. More importantly, however, he provided direction and guidance over those forty-three years to literally hundreds of people who sought his advice. He refused no one ... Buddhist, Christian, Jewish, Hindu, Muslim ... these distinctions didn't matter. He saw each one as a human being who was struggling to live the best life that they could. He didn't judge; he listened. And he offered advice. The impact that he has had on the lives of so many people is truly immeasurable. And the sacrifices he made to do this are equally great. He did not exploit his students for money. He did not amass buckets of cash to use for his personal use or to send back to his home country. He did not build himself a luxurious house or buy an expensive car. He did not travel the globe on sightseeing trips. No. He used whatever donations he received for dharma purposes only. He started out over 40 years ago in Los Angeles living in very humble circumstances and he lives today, forty-plus years later, at the age of 90 years, as humbly as he did those forty years ago.

I close with the following story told by one of Lama Dorje's students. I was there. This happened. It illustrates the great love and good-heartedness that Lama Karma Dorje has generated in the hearts of his students.

> *On rare occasions, an event takes place that one never would have imagined might happen. This particular happening occurred at the end of a workday on the Kagyu Mila Guru stupa in Questa. The little KMG shrine room was packed with workers. I remember some make-shift chairs and benches on the inside of the room with cement dust covering the floor and most of the people, including Lama Dorje. Anna Rubyan was there and with her beautiful voice, she began to sing. We all sang with her. We sang the lovely song she had written that says: With a beam of love, I touch the heart of my sister (or brother) followed by their name. The verse was repeated with the name of each person that was crammed*

*in shoulder to shoulder in that room. I was sitting across the space from Lama Dorje when we sang, "**With a beam of love, I touch the heart of Lama Dorje**." Tears were rolling down his cheeks. We were all one family, one truly loving family. It was an incredible moment. There was no separation. We were all one.*

-   *Anna R.*

What a great gift and what a great blessing is this special being called Lama Karma Dorje!

GLOSSARY

GLOSSARY OF TERMS

1. **Bodhisattva:** Bodhisattva is the Sanskrit name given to one who lives life and bases actions on the wish to attain enlightenment for the benefit of all living things. Bodhisattvas are sometimes referred to as the "Sons and Daughters" of the Buddha.

2. **Chenrezig:** The Lord of Compassion, also known by the Sanskrit name Avalokiteshvara, is the embodiment of the compassion of all the Buddhas. Chenrezig meditation practice is one of the main practices at Lama Dorje's Centers.

3. **Dharma:** The teachings of the Buddha. This word is sometimes translated as "the truth."

4. **Dorje:** A dorje or "vajra" is a Tibetan Buddhist symbol and the ritual object used to represent the indestructible, diamond-like hardness of enlightenment.

5. **Enlightenment:** The state of Buddhahood characterized by the accumulation of merit and wisdom and the removal of all obscurations.

6. **Kangyur:** The ***Kangyur*** or "Translated Words" consists of 108 volumes of the complete teachings of the Buddha as they were spoken by the Buddha himself. All texts presumably once had Sanskrit originals, but the Kangyur as we know it today is written in the Tibetan language. Copies of the Kangyur have become extremely rare since many of them were destroyed after the Chinese invaded Tibet.

7. **Karma:** Karma is a Sanskrit word meaning "action." It refers to a cycle of cause and effect that is an important concept in many Eastern religions, particularly in Hinduism and Buddhism. It is similar to the concept that we "reap what we sow." Karma is not set in stone. It is not out of your control. It means that the steps of your life, your spiritual development and your personality are directly molded by your thoughts and actions.

8. **Lama:** In Tibetan Buddhism, lama refers to one who is a spiritual leader. Originally, the term was used to translate "guru" (Sanskrit: "venerable one") and thus applicable only to heads of monasteries. The term is now extended out of courtesy to any respected monk or priest but most often only to those who have completed a three-year retreat. Some lamas are considered reincarnations of their predecessors. These are termed *tulku* lamas, as distinguished from "developed" lamas, who have won respect because of the high level of spiritual development they have achieved in their present lifetime. The highest lineage of reincarnate lamas is that of Dalai Lama, who was, until 1959 when he went into exile, the temporal ruler of Tibet.

9. **Paramitas:** The Sanskrit word *"paramita"* means *"crossing over"* or *"going beyond"* mundane knowledge and activity to transcendent understanding. The practice of the Six Paramitas is the principal practice of a Bodhisattva. The Six Paramitas are generosity, ethical discipline, patience, diligence, concentration and wisdom.

10. **Pecha:** ***Pecha*** is a Tibetan word meaning "book", but refers, in particular, to the traditional Tibetan loose-leaf books such as the Kangyur, Tengyur, and sadhanas many of which are used for meditation purposes. See an example of a page from a *pecha* in the Appendices.

11. **Puja:** Puja is a Sanskrit word that means reverence, honor, homage, adoration and worship. It refers to a worship ritual performed by Buddhists to offer devotional homage and prayer to one or more deities, to host and honor a guest, or to spiritually celebrate an event. It may honor or celebrate the presence of special guests, or their memories after they die. Puja is also the loving offering of light, flowers, and water or food to the divine.

12. **Refuge:** Refuge is a place that provides protection or shelter from danger and distress. *Refuge* in *Buddhism* is about changing our state of mind. This means deepening our understanding of what gives life purpose and what will bring us happiness. When we're children, we take refuge in our parents. We believe that no matter what goes wrong, Mom and Dad can fix it. As adults, we might take refuge in authority figures, our career, or our social identity. But when we start to look deeper, it becomes clear that none of these things can help us ultimately. In Buddhism, practitioners take refuge in the Three Jewels: the Buddha, Dharma and Sangha. Traditionally, the *Buddha* refers to the historical Buddha. However, it can also refer to your teacher, whoever in your life most represents for you the consciousness of an enlightened being. *Dharma* is the path and the Buddhist teachings that guide us towards true wisdom and the awakening of compassion. The *Sangha* is traditionally any group of ordained monks or nuns. *Your* sangha, on the other hand, might be the group of people with whom you study dharma or meditate. A group of people who are on the path together can support, encourage, and inspire each other.

13. **Sangha:** The word "sangha" refers to the community of practitioners of Buddhism in much the same way that the word "congregation" is used to describe those attending traditional church services. Sometimes this term is used to mean the ordained sangha such as lamas, monks and nuns, and sometimes it is used more broadly to mean all practitioners including lay persons.

14. **Stupa:** The word stupa is a Sanskrit word meaning "heap." A stupa is an important form of Buddhist architecture. At its simplest, a stupa is a dirt burial mound faced with stone. The shape of the stupa came to be associated with the body of the Buddha. Stupas have been built all over the world as representations of his form or memorials to his deeds.

15. **Thangka:** A thangka is a Tibetan Buddhist painting often depicting a Buddhist deity, scene or mandala. Thangkas are usually painted on silk and mounted on a textile backing somewhat in the style of Chinese scroll paintings.

16. **Three Jewels:** The Three Jewels are the three objects of refuge: the Buddha, the Dharma and the Sangha. They are called "Jewels" because they are both rare and precious.

17. **Tsa-Tsa:** A small clay image of a stupa about six inches in height. The upper portion of the tsa-tsa is painted gold and the bottom portion a bright red. Prayers and mantras are written and inserted inside of each tsa-tsa.

www.kimcuongthua.org

18. **Tsen:** The maroon-colored shawl-like robe worn by ordained monks and nuns.

APPENDICES

APPENDICES

1. **HIS HOLINESS KARMAPA** – Leader of the Karma Kagyu Lineage

2. **HIS HOLINESS KALU RINPOCHE** – Lama Dorje's Teacher

3. **VENERABLE WANGCHEN RINPOCHE** – Biographical Information

4. **LAMA SARAH HARDING** – Biographical Information

5. **DR. FRED COOPER** – Biographical Information

6. **KSK STUPA** – Detailed Description and listing of paintings on the walls.

7. **SAMPLE PAGES** from Tibetan Buddhist text (*Pecha*).

HIS HOLINESS
THE 16ᵀᴴ GYALWA KARMAPA

The sixteenth Gyalwa Karmapa, Rangjung Rigpe Dorje, was the spiritual leader of the Karma Kagyu lineage of Tibetan Buddhism. Followers believed him to be part of the oldest line of reincarnate lamas in Vajrayana Buddhism, known as the Karmapas, whose coming was predicted by the Buddha.

Under his leadership, the Karma Kagyu lineage not only survived the escape from Tibet of most of the high Buddhist teachers — but thrived. The Karma Kagyu lineage spread all around the world. The Buddhist monasteries, institutes, and centers that the 16th Karmapa established grew and now offer Buddhist teachings to people in India, Asia, and across the West.

The 16th Karmapa was a great master who demonstrated intuitive wisdom, joy, and loving-kindness, his compassionate activity for other beings was limitless. He was such a highly respected teacher across the Himalayas — including to the royal families of Sikkim and Bhutan — that masters of the other lineages would also call upon him for help and advice. His main monastery was Rumtek Monastery in Sikkim. Rumtek is where Lama Karma Dorje received his monastic training.

VERY VENERABLE KALU RINPOCHE

Kyabje Dorje Chang Kalu Rinpoche was a yogi, scholar, and one of the great meditation masters of the Buddhist tradition. His teachings were sought by lamas of all four schools of Buddhism in Tibet. A senior Meditation Master of the Karma Kagyu tradition and lineage holder of the Shangpa Kagyu sect, Kalu Rinpoche was among the first Tibetan Buddhist monks to spread the Dharma to the West and establish Dharma centers and facilities for Westerners.

Kalu Rinpoche was born in 1905 in eastern Tibet in the Kham region. Rinpoche's parents were students of the great teacher Jamgön Kontrul Lodrö Thaye. Both of Kalu Rinpoche's parents were devoted to practice and undertook a religious retreat immediately after their marriage. Kalu Rinpoche began his formal studies at Palpung Monastery at the age of thirteen. At sixteen, Kalu Rinpoche entered Kunzang Dechen Osal Ling, the retreat center founded by Jamgön Kongtrul Lodrö Thaye and completed the traditional three-year retreat. At age twenty-five, he departed for an extended retreat in the desolate mountains of Kham. Wandering without possessions, taking shelter in caves and under cliffs, seeking and needing no human company, he intended to spend the rest of his life in solitude. But after spending twelve years meditating in this way, he saw that it would benefit all beings greatly if he were to return and teach the Dharma.

In 1971, Kalu Rinpoche began traveling to Europe and North America, where he established numerous Dharma centers. He was the first Tibetan master to build facilities for Westerners to undertake the traditional three-year retreat. During his 1986 visit, he consecrated the KSK Stupa in Santa Fe. He also announced that due to his advanced age, he would probably not be able to come back again. He invited everyone to visit him at his monastery in Sonada, where he would be residing. After several more years of extensive Dharma activity in many countries, he returned to his monastery in Sonada. On May 10, 1989, in a state of profound meditation, Kalu Rinpoche departed and left for the pure realms. Kalu Rinpoche was Lama Karma Dorje's teacher and retreat master.

VENERABLE WANGCHEN RINPOCHE

Venerable Wangchen Rinpoche is a Tibetan Buddhist teacher. He was born in India and at the age of seven, he became a monk at Sonada monastery in Northeast India near Darjeeling. This was the monastery of his root guru Dorje Chang Kalu Rinpoche, one of the foremost spiritual teachers of the 20th century. Wangchen Rinpoche is the heart son and the spiritual heir of his Guru's lineage, known as the lineage of the Golden Teachings. This unique lineage is officially known as the Shangpa Kagyu and was started by two enlightened women from India, Sukhasiddhi and Niguma. Wangchen Rinpoche lived with his Guru who loved him very much. As Kalu Rinpoche traveled around the world, he always brought Wangchen Rinpoche with him.

Wangchen Rinpoche started his three-year retreat at fifteen (according to the Western calendar) and began his teaching career in Europe when he was nineteen. He lived in Belgium for four years and taught all over Europe. In 1987, Wangchen Rinpoche moved to Los Angeles when he was twenty-four years old.

In addition to his responsibilities as lineage holder of the Golden Teachings, Wangchen Rinpoche has become the greatest living master of Nyungne practice, a practice based on Kriya and Acharya Buddhist yoga tantra. Wangchen Rinpoche recently completed his commitment to do 1000 Nyungne. This rigorous, two-day fasting practice of 1000-armed Avalokiteshvara (Chenrezig) is a powerful purification. The first day one can eat a single vegetarian meal at midday and the second day is a 24-hour silent, dry fast.

When asked why he made this commitment, Rinpoche responded, "I wanted to be a role model for my students. I wanted them to follow in my footsteps and be confident that they could achieve their goals. Making a commitment is so important; I wanted to show that to my students and to everyone who wishes to follow the dharma path. You must keep practicing. There is no stopping until you reach Buddhahood."

Among Buddhist teachers, Wangchen Rinpoche is unusual in his command of English, despite having no formal training. As well as teaching around the world, Wangchen Rinpoche is responsible for three monasteries in Tibet, two for monks and one for nuns. The largest monastery has 300 monks, a Buddhist college, and a three-year retreat center.

Rinpoche's main center, Ser Cho Ling, "The Realm of the Golden Teachings" is in North Fork, California, just south of Yosemite National Park. The center's website is www.sercholing.org.

LAMA SARAH HARDING

Lama Sarah Harding is an exceptional woman. She has been studying and practicing Buddhism since 1974, and has been teaching and translating since completing a three-year retreat in 1980 under the guidance of Kyabjé Kalu Rinpoché. For over twenty-five years, she was an associate professor at Naropa University in Boulder, Colorado where she currently resides. She has been a fellow of the Tsadra Foundation since 2000. She specializes in Tibetan Buddhist literature with a focus on tantric practice. Her publications include *Creation and Completion*; *The Treasury of Knowledge: Esoteric Instructions*; *Niguma, Lady of Illusion*; and two volumes on Chö and Shijé from *The Treasury of Precious Instructions*.

Sarah completed the first three-year retreat for westerners at Kagyu Ling, France, in 1976–1980 under the tutelage of Kalu Rinpoche. She was one of the first western women to complete such a retreat. Sarah describes those years as follows:

> *I met my teacher Kalu Rinpoche at his monastery near Darjeeling, India around 1972. I immediately launched into his program of practice through daily teachings in his room with a small group of westerners, in the midst of the usual life of an all-male monastery. One event that struck me was the sudden "liberation", as it is called, of a three-year retreat that had been going on there unbeknownst to me. I was extremely impressed*

by the monks that emerged. Later, when Kalu Rinpoche announced the first retreat for westerners, I immediately applied and was not-so-immediately accepted! I learned Tibetan, did the preliminary practices, accumulated the money, helped to build the retreat facilities at the Center in France and entered retreat in 1976, along with seven other women. There was only one nun among us. The men were similarly ensconced a short distance away. Rinpoche had not been deterred by criticism from other lamas for assigning women the same practice program as the men, but he did truly wish that everyone would ordain as monastic and never gave up trying.

When the retreat ended in 1980, the first thing that happened was that Rinpoche had each of us give a Dharma talk there at the center in France. So, the message was clear: we would be teaching, even though no one had that in mind when they entered retreat ... at least not the women. I can't speak for the men. The next thing was that we were all to accompany Rinpoche on a tour of the Centers around France, sitting on the stage with him in our maroon robes and advertised as "the first thirteen occidental lamas." Rinpoche was clearly proud of this achievement, and we basked in the glory!

After she completed her retreat and at the request of her teacher Kalu Rinpoche, Sarah moved to Los Angeles to assist Lama Dorje. In 1981, Sarah moved to Santa Fe, New Mexico, with Lama Dorje who had been requested by Kalu Rinpoche to start a Tibetan Buddhist Center there now known as Kagyu Shenpen Kunchab. From 1981 to 1992, Sarah served at Kagyu Shenpen Kunchab as a translator, teacher and advisor to Lama Dorje. At this same time, she was a wife and mother of two children.

Sarah was a founding member of Kalu Rinpoche's International Translation Group established in 1987 and has taught the Tibetan language to hundreds of students over the years, including creating a popular Tibetan language correspondence course. In 1992, she joined the faculty of Naropa Institute and taught there for twenty-six years until her retirement in 2018. She continues her written translation work with the Tsadra Foundation from her home in Boulder, Colorado. She is the author of many books on Tibetan Buddhism, most recently the book *Four Tibetan Lineages*, presenting some of Tibetan Buddhism's most transformative teachings on meditative practices.

DR. FRED COOPER

Dr. Fred Cooper is a quantum field theorist who was a Ph.D. student of the Nobel Prize winning Physicist Sheldon Lee Glashow, one of the inventors of the Standard Model of Elementary Particle Physics. He has written over 300 published research papers and is best known as one of the founders of the fields of Supersymmetry and Quantum Mechanics and Non-equilibrium Quantum Field Theory. From 2002-2009, Fred was the Program Director for Theoretical Physics at the National Science Foundation. Currently he is on the External Faculty of the Santa Fe Institute. He has been a student of HE Tai Situ Rinpoche since 1981 and received from him the entire transmission of the Nyedon Gyamtso (Ocean of Definitive Meaning) by the 9th Karmapa. He has also received direct Mahamudra transmissions from HE the first Kalu Rinpoche, VV Mingyur Rinpoche and Traleg Kyabgon Rinpoche. He has had Dzogchen transmissions from VV Mingyur Rinpoch.

Fred has been teaching meditation at Buddhist centers affiliated with HE Kalu Rinpoche for over 30 years and he is the President of Kagyu Shenpen Kunchab Buddhist Center in Santa Fe, NM.

KAGYU SHENPEN KUCHAB BODHI STUPA
Santa Fe, New Mexico

Detailed Description

In the Tibetan tradition, the stupa demonstrates the entire path of inner, outer and secret levels. It is a symbol of Dharmakaya, the universal principle of all consciousness. Upon seeing a stupa, a deep imprint in the viewer's mind arouses Bodhicitta that can ripen into enlightenment. It is said that rainbow-like visions of the stupa appeared to those who witnessed the major events in the Buddha's life. His enlightened actions purified the uninformed fixations of the moment and universal consciousness manifested as pure form in the sky. Later, replicas of these visions were built and venerated, becoming the earliest Buddhist shrines. They proliferated in many cultures in various adapted styles and often enshrined the relics of great saints, focusing people's devotion. The stupa is believed to be capable of tremendous Buddha activity, such as drawing the Buddhas to earth, speeding the rebirth of lamas, promoting longevity and creating harmony.By building this stupa, the world is offered a powerful blessing for peace and happiness. Individuals may find calm and inspiration by meditation in and around the stupa. If they are inspired to follow the path of compassion, they may find great fulfillment.

Upon entering the KSK Bodhi Stupa, one's attention is first drawn to the front wall. A large statue of the Shakyamuni Buddha sits nobly in the center. This Buddha turned the wheel of dharma in 500 BC. The heart of the Buddhists teachings is the viewpoint that all sentient beings have Buddha nature, even though it may be obscured by fixation on ego. This Buddha nature is represented by the small figures of Samantabhadra Samantabhadri at the top. Buddha nature is said to naturally manifest as the five wisdoms that are represented by the five Buddha families. Starting on the right of the southern wall these families are as follow:

- **Akshobya** of the Vajra family who represents mirror-like wisdom.
- **Amitabha** of the Lotus family represents the wisdom of discriminating awareness.
- **Vairochana** od the Buddha family who represents universal consciousness.
- **Amoghasiddhi** of the Karma family representing all-encompassing wisdom.
- **Ratnasambhava** of the Ratna family who represents the wisdom of equanimity.

When these qualities manifest in sentient beings, the true nature of mind emerges.

The teachings of the Buddha descended through various lineages that are represented on the walls of the stupa.

EAST WALL:

To the left of the Buddha on the East wall are representations of the Shangpa Kagyu Lineage, whose present lineage holder is Yangsi Kalu Rinpoche, including Guru Rinpoche (Padmasambhava) who brought Buddhism to Tibet and Khyungpo Naljor, the founder and first lineage holder of the Shanpa Kagyu lineage. He took full ordination with Geshe Langri Tangpa and travelled seven times to India from Tibet, bringing back many teachings from masters such as Niguma, Sukhasiddhi, Maitripa and Vajrasana. He made his seat in a place called Shang in the Tsang region of Tibet. He was therefore known as the Lama Shangpa. He founded over one hundred monasteries in Tibet and taught tirelessly, manifesting many miracles. He is said to have lived for 150 years.

The Shangpa lineage started in Tibet with Khyungpo Naljor. In the 10th century he went on a pilgrimage to India and studied with many gurus. His two main teachers were the dakinis Sukhasiddhi and Niguma. As the story goes, he brought gold with him to make offerings. He found Niguma in a charnel ground in the sky surrounded by many wrathful dakinis, He prepared a mandala offering of five cups of gold dust. Niguma kicked the offering into the air saying she had no need of gold because when the pure view of all appearances is obtained, the whole world is gold. Then Niguma gave Khyungpo Naljor the "five golden doctrines" of the Shangpa Kagyu teachings. She likened these doctrines to a tree. The six roots are the six yogas of Niguma: heat, illusory body, dream state, sheer clarity, transference and bardo. The main truck is the tradition of Mahamudra. The three branches are the three methods of carrying one's understanding in meditation into daily activities. The flowers are the practice of development and completion of white and red dakinins. The fruit is the wisdom of deathlessness, changelessness and body.

Additional teachings were given to Khyungpo Naljor by Sukasiddhi. Sukasiddhi was banished from her home for giving her poor family's last container of rice to a begging monk. She wandered around and eventually earned a living making beer. Virupa, an Indian Mahasiddhi, was very fond of her beer and became her teacher. After three years of study and contemplation, Sukasiddhi obtained the rainbow body and the 60-year-old woman looked like a beautiful 16-year-old girl. She lived in many isolated places and appears throughout time in various forms to people of appropriate realization.

The Shangpa lineage contains many famous yogis. One of most famous is the 15th century Tangtong Gyalpo, who developed a method of forging iron and was the inventor of the iron chain link bridge. His major activity was connecting Tibet's bridges and roads. He had a vision of the whole of Tibet as the body of a demoness lying prostrate on the ground. At various points on her body, the demoness had certain energy potentials that could be enhanced by creating a way for pilgrims.

Tantong Gyalpo also composed the Chenrezig practice, the main meditation used at KSK Center. His teachings were transmitted through many disciples and preserved by the great 19th century teacher Jamgon Kongtrul Lodro Taye. Jamgon Kongtrul included them in his *Treasury of Key Instructions*. He was also one of the founders of the Rime movement whose intent was to teach and preserve the teachings of all lineages in a non-sectarian way.

Also on the East Wall are the representations of the following:
1. **Guru Rinpoche** (*Padmasambhava)* who brought Buddhism to Tibet.
2. **Green Tara**, the female Boddhisattva of Compassion,
3. **Vajrasattva (Dorje Sempa)** who represents the primordial nature of mind.
4. **Vajrayogini** surrounded by the dakinis of the Buddha families
5. **Machik Lobdron** an 11th-century female believed to have been an emanation of Tara. She introduced the practice of Chod designed to cut through neuroses.

WEST WALL:

The Karma Kagyu lineage is represented on the west wall of the shrine room. Marpa, the first Tibetan in the lineage, went to India many times and brought back Buddhist teachings to Tibet. The main teachings of the lineage came from Naropa, who was Marpa's teacher and the author of the famous *Six Yogas of Naropa* and the Mahahmudra teachings. Marpa's chief disciple was Jetsun Milarepa who became one of Tibet's greatest yogis. Marpa's most famous student was Dusum Kyenpa who became the first Karmapa. The Karmapa reincarnated in successive generations and started the Karma Kaygu lineage.

Also on the west wall are paintings of the Five Buddha families.

1. **Akshobya** – Vajra family – representing Mirror-Like Wisdom
2. **Amitabha** – Lotus family – representing Discriminating Awareness
3. **Vairochana** – Buddha family – representing Dharmadhatu Wisdom
4. **Amogasiddhi** – Karma family – rerpresenting All-Empowering Wisdom
5. **Ratnasambhava** – Ratna family – representing Equanimity

The primary figure on the West Wall is Chenrezig (Avilokiteshvara), Lord of Compassion and a deity much revered in the Tibetan Buddhist tradition. The Karma Kagyu Lineage is also represented on the West wall including:

1. **Marpa** – the first Tibetan in the lineage
2. **Tilopa** – Marpa's student and a gifted teacher
3. **Naropa** – Professor at Nalanda University who authored the *Six Yogas of Naropa* and Mahamudra teachings
4. **Milarepa** – one of Tibet's greatest yogis and poets
5. **Gampopa** – Milarepa's most famous student
6. **Dusum Khyenpa** – the first Karmapa of the Karma Kagyu lineage

NORTH WALL:

The paintings on the North Wall represent many of the protective deities in the Tibetan tradition. These include the Bodhisattvas Manjushri [wisdom], Vajrapani [power], and Avilokiteshvara [compassion]. Other protective deities on that wall are Chagdrukpa [6-arm Mahakala] and Bernakchen [2-armed Mahakala] along with the five main Shangpa Kagyu Deities: Chakrasambhara, Hevajra, Mahamaya, Yamantaka and Guhyasamaya.

SAMPLE PECHA PAGES

Pecha is a Tibetan word meaning "book." It refers in particular to the traditional Tibetan loose-leaf books used for meditation purposes. Except for brief periods during the practice, Tibetan Buddhist meditation is not a silent meditation but is instead, the chanting of prayers. [14] These prayers are contained in small books called pechas. In traditional Tibetan practice, these prayers are written entirely in Tibetan characters, however, the format of these pechas has been adapted for non-Tibetans by including several additional lines.

1. The first line in the text is written in Tibetan characters.

2. The second line in the text is the phonetical sound of each of the Tibetan words.

3. The third line of the text is the English translation of the Tibetan words.

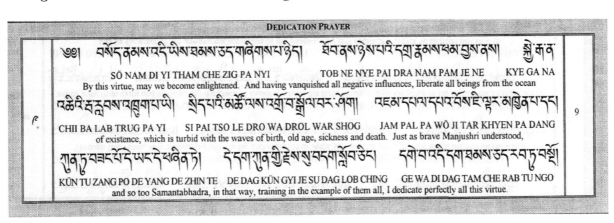

DEDICATION PRAYER

SÖ NAM DI YI THAM CHE ZIG PA NYI   TOB NE NYE PAI DRA NAM PAM JE NE   KYE GA NA
By this virtue, may we become enlightened. And having vanquished all negative influences, liberate all beings from the ocean

CHII BA LAB TRUG PA YI   SI PAI TSO LE DRO WA DROL WAR SHOG   JAM PAL PA WÖ JI TAR KHYEN PA DANG
of existence, which is turbid with the waves of birth, old age, sickness and death. Just as brave Manjushri understood,

KÜN TU ZANG PO DE YANG DE ZHIN TE   DE DAG KÜN GYI JE SU DAG LOB CHING   GE WA DI DAG TAM CHE RAB TU NGO
and so too Samantabhadra, in that way, training in the example of them all, I dedicate perfectly all this virtue.

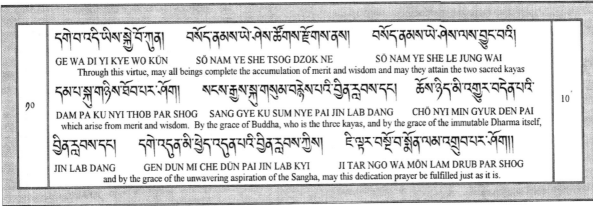

GE WA DI YI KYE WO KÜN   SÖ NAM YE SHE TSOG DZOK NE   SÖ NAM YE SHE LE JUNG WAI
Through this virtue, may all beings complete the accumulation of merit and wisdom and may they attain the two sacred kayas

DAM PA KU NYI THOB PAR SHOG   SANG GYE KU SUM NYE PAI JIN LAB DANG   CHÖ NYI MIN GYUR DEN PAI
which arise from merit and wisdom. By the grace of Buddha, who is the three kayas, and by the grace of the immutable Dharma itself,

JIN LAB DANG   GEN DUN MI CHE DÜN PAI JIN LAB KYI   JI TAR NGO WA MÖN LAM DRUB PAR SHOG
and by the grace of the unwavering aspiration of the Sangha, may this dedication prayer be fulfilled just as it is.

---

[14] *There are several Tibetan Buddhist meditations such as "shin nay" that are, in fact, almost entirely silent practices.*

ACKNOWLEDGMENTS

ACKNOWLEDGMENTS

The building of a stupa is not an overnight event nor is it the work of a single individual. The stupas that are described in this book were the work of many people over lots of time often measuring three or four years. The people who worked on these stupas were regular and ordinary people. They had regular jobs that demanded their effort and time, they had families that needed and received their care and attention, and they had homes of their own that needed repairs and renovations. What was not ordinary or regular about these people is the time, the effort and the commitment that they made to build stupas in addition to the other demands on their time and energy. I have listed here some of their names with the briefest of descriptions.

KAGYU SHENPEN KUNCHAB
Santa Fe, New Mexico

Jeremy (Jerry) Morell – Under the direction and with the assistance of Lama Karma Dorje, Jerry was the Lead Builder of the KSK Stupa. Jerry had previously built a retreat center for Kalu Rinpoche in France.

Ken and Sally Maynard – This couple were the coordinators of the first KSK Tibetan Buddhist Center in Santa Fe, NM. They hosted Lama Dorje when he first came to Santa Fe in their home on Irvine Street, which also served as the Center's first meditation space.

Cynthia Moku – Cynthia is a gifted artist who worked tirelessly on paintings inside the KSK stupa shrine room in Santa Fe, New Mexico and in the KMG stupa in Questa, New Mexico. She is trained in both western painting and drawing techniques as well as eastern art forms. She has completed large scale art pieces in the Himalayan Buddhist tradition for more than forty years. These projects include interior mural painting projects for three major stupas in the United States: the KDK Bodhi Stupa in Santa Fe, New Mexico, the Kagyu Mila Guru stupa in Questa, New Mexico, and the Great Stupa of Dharmakaya at the Shambala Mountain Center in Colorado.

Cynthia met Kyabje Kalu Rinpoche in 1973. Under his prompting and instruction, she began a life-long study, meditation training, and practice in the art of emblematic illustrated dharma. Commissioned by both Tibetan and American spiritual teachers, her paintings reside across the globe. This incudes the seminal painting of the Protector *Chagdrukpa Mahakala*, acquired by the Denver Art Museum. Consecrated by His Holiness, the Dalai Lama, this piece has the distinction of being the first thangka painting in the Karma Ghadri style acquired by a major American museum for its permanent collection. Cynthia is a professor at Naropa Institute in Boulder, Colorado, where she has taught painting and design for many years.

Cynthia was also the primary artist for the paintings inside the Kagyu Mila Guru stupa in Questa, New Mexico. She was not only the lead artist but she used the opportunity to teach many members of the KMG community and her own students the art of Tibetan Buddhist painting. Her work and her commitment made her a beloved member of the KMG sangha. Cynthia's contributions to the many stupas and other Buddhist buildings are monumental and enduring.

Sanje Elliot – Sanje is a gifted painter and a member of the sangha in Portland Oregon. He was one of the artists responsible for the beautiful paintings inside the KSK stupa shrine room. Sanje has been practicing Tibetan arts since 1974. He studied with numerous Tibetan artists in Darjeeling and Kathmandu. He also studied at Lewis & Clark College and the Museum Art School in Portland, Oregon. He is the former Head of the Art Department at Naropa University and a painting instructor at Portland State University. He is the author of several books including *Tibetan Sacred Art* and *Tibetan Calligraphy*. His paintings, calligraphy and thangka paintings have been shown internationally.

There were many other people who helped and donated to the building of this wonderful stupa and they deserve acknowledgment. I was unable to find any records of their names and contributions. Though unnamed in this text, they know who they are and they know the blessings they have received from their generous and heartfelt contributions. They are all hereby acknowledged.

KAGYU DEKYI CHOLING
Taos, New Mexico

Norbert Ubechel – Under the direction of and with the assistance of Lama Karma Dorje, Norbert was the Lead Builder on the KDC stupa in Taos, New Mexico. Norbert is a successful builder and businessman who is known for the beautiful and original corbels and vigas that he designed and made for southwest style architecture buildings.

Gal and Janice Tabib - Gal and Janice are two of Lama Dorje's earliest students and helpers and among the first residents to build a home in Tres Orejas. Among other things, Gal hauled water every week to the KDC stupa worksite for the builders to use. Gal is a nurse and Janice is a gifted photographer.

Ken McNamara – Ken was one of the earliest helpers at the KDC site. In addition to working on the stupa, he continues to this day to help with the many buildings that have been constructed at KDC. Ken works in the technology field.

David Bates – David has become the Lead Builder for Lama Dorje, not only at the KDC site in Taos but also with other building projects at the KSK Center in Santa Fe. He is a general contractor who continues to build homes and other structures in Taos, New Mexico with an emphasis on sustainability, such as solar power.

Cassandra Bates – Cassandra is another of Lama Dorje's earliest and most devoted students at KDC. Along with her friend, Pam Parker, she organized the work force for various projects at KDC and with her tireless energy, kept these projects moving along. In addition, Cassandra and Pam were the "chief cooks and bottler washers" who fed both Lama Dorje and the crew who were working at KDC. Cassandra was the owner of a beautiful and successful retail shop in Taos, NM called Wabi Sabi.

Pam Parker – Pam is one of Lama Dorje's longest and most senior members of the KDC sangha. Along with Cassandra, Pam was an organizer and a driving force to keep projects moving at KDC. She was also the chief cook and bottlewasher! She is an excellent cook as both Lama Dorje and the KDC sangha can attest. Along with several helpers, Pam continues to this day to prepare food each week for Lama Dorje and the KDC sangha. Pam is a talented businesswoman in her own right who owns a very beautiful and successful business in Taos, New Mexico called Taos Gems and Minerals. Her shop is a true delight just to visit!

Alice Zorthian – Alice is a steady member of the KDC sangha who is a quiet, behind the scenes helper who makes herself available whenever and wherever she is needed at the Center. She is a gifted artist and a successful real estate agent in Taos, NM.

Ruth Fahrbach – Ruth is a steady and devoted member of the KDC sangha. She makes herself enthusiastically available to help where she is needed. She is also a jazz singer and a bit of a resident philosopher, happily offering advice from her more senior status to younger sangha members who value her experience. She is a delight to be around!

Greg King - Greg is another steady and devoted student of Lama Dorje. Greg is one of those special people who without a lot of splash or fanfare quietly seems to be available and helpful wherever he is needed.

Virginia Oppenheimer - Virginia is one of Lama Dorje's most constant and longtime students. She lives in Santa Fe and is vice-president of the KSK Center. For more years than one can count, she arises early, goes out to the KSK stupa, picks up Lama Dorje around 7 am and drives him up to the KDC Center in Taos, about 80 miles away. In addition to Lama Dorje, she also brings coffee and Dunkin' Donuts for the sangha! Virginia's steady and strong commitment to Lama Dorje and the dharma community is an inspiring gift to all.

Lama Yeshe and Lama Tsering – This husband-and-wife duo are fully ordained lamas. Both have completed the three-year retreat. For many years they divided their time between their home in Oregon and their home in Tres Orejas. In addition to working on the building projects at the KDC Center, they also provided help and counsel to those building the Kyang Tsik chorten in Questa.

KAGYU MILA GURU
Questa, New Mexico

Charles Dillon – Charles was the Lead Builder and General Contractor for the KMG stupa. In addition to coordinating all the material and workers required for this project, he also handled the budget and the permits and inspections that were necessary. Charles was also a successful General Contractor in his own right. From the time he agreed to the stupa project until today, he remains an enthusiastic worker and supporter. The KMG stupa could not have been completed without Charles.

Margy Dillon – Until her passing, Margy worked side by side with her husband Charles, providing whatever backup support he needed or the project needed. She also worked physically on the stupa, hauling concrete block, mixing cement and whatever was required. Margy was a gifted gardener with a degree in Horticulture.

It was and is her efforts that are responsible for some of the beautiful planting around the stupa and stupa site.

Jennifer Dillon (Laabes)
Evan Dillon

These are Charles and Margy's children. Children were an important part of building the KMG stupa and Jennifer and Evan were no exception. Today, Jennifer, who has a degree in Landscape Architecture, owns and operates a successful nursery and landscaping business in Taos, NM. Evan is a counselor in Phoenix, Arizona.

STEVE and ANNA RACICOT – This dedicated duo were two of the most reliable and steady workers on the KMG stupa project. Neither rain, nor wind, nor storm kept this couple from arriving early at the stupa site and working earnestly and continuously all day long. There was no task too difficult nor any job too menial for them to handle. Steve was especially daring on some of the high-rise tasks required to complete the highest parts of the stupa building. Steve and Anna are successful publishers of both books and magazines and to this day continue their work with dream yoga.

Katherine Racicot (Florey)
Joseph Racicot

These are Steve and Anna's children who helped build the stupa. Lama Dorje was especially interested in teaching the children "building techniques" using scraps of wood and concrete block to illustrate his point. Today, Katherine is the Manager of the Questa Credit Union in Questa, NM and Joseph excels and works in IT and computer graphics. He currently manages the Museum Store at the Harwood Museum of Art in Taos, New Mexico.

TIMOTHY and CONNIE LONG – Timothy and Connie worked diligently and consistently on the building of the stupa. They were especially helpful with the carpentry and woodworking portions of the stupa because they are, in their own right, gifted woodworkers. They have a successful and well-established business called North Star Toys which makes, sells and distributes hand-made wooden toys for children throughout the country. Timothy is also a talented musician who plays enthusiastically in the local band as well as teaching "drumming" skills to many students.

Claire Long (Cote)
Joan Long

Timothy and Connie's two daughters were always welcome and helpful participants at the stupa site. The presence of the children was always a delightful reminder of the continuity of the blessings of the stupa. Claire and Joan are both gifted artists and loving mothers today.

HILECE ROSE AND MICHAEL WALSH – Hilece and Michael were and still are steady and deeply committed builders of the KMG Stupa. They both serve as officers of Earth Journey, Inc., a non-profit corporation that manages and operates the stupa and related buildings at that site. They also serve on the board of the Herman Redick Trust which manages the buildings and property left to the Lorien community when Herman Rednick passed away. To this day they remain the primary custodians and caretakers of the stupa and the various buildings surrounding it that have been completed since the stupa was built. Hilece is both a nurse and a pastoral counselor. Hilece is also the person who first introduced me to Lama Karma Dorje. Michael is a very talented, professional photographer and an organic farmer.

Christopher Rose

Christopher is Hilece's son who was one of the children always present for the stupa building. Christopher, along with his wife Ivonne, both completed the three-year Buddhist retreat and are now successful teachers worldwide, known as Lama Zopa and Lama Yeshe. Their website is prajnafire.com and their teachings are on Instagram at karmayeshechodron. It has been a moving and meaningful experience to see one of the "youthful stupa builders" move deeply onto the Dharma path.

GABRIELLE HERBERTSON – Gabrielle has a light, fairy-like presence that lent a delightful note to the stupa project. But her fairy-like quality belied the fact that she was a very diligent and hard worker. From start to finish, she was always there. She was and is a gifted and creative teacher and poet. She is also one of the always reliable, often behind-the-scenes, custodians of the Stupa and the buildings that surround it. Gabrielle was Cynthia Moku's main helper with the paintings on the interior of the KMG Stupa.

Gabriel Herbertson
David Herbertson

Gabe and David were two more of the children in the local community who participated in the stupa project. It was always fun to watch these children on the sidelines listening to a building lesson from Lama Dorje or simply being kids and throwing dirt around!

RACHEL SAYRE – Rachel is a long-time, well-loved member of the Lorien community and was an active participant in the building of the stupa. During a portion of the stupa construction, Rachel lived in southern California where she was Vice-President at Mira Costa College in Oceanside, California. She has an extensive background in organizational skills and community participation projects and a cut-to-the-chase sense of humor that kept us all on our toes and laughing at the same time!

RAFAEL WISEMAN – Rafael lived across the road from the stupa project and lent many of his generous and neighborly skills to building the stupa. Perhaps his most tangible contribution was that he supplied water. There was no water at the stupa site and Raphael allowed us to run a hose from his house to the building site, making mixing cement possible. Raphael is a gifted musician who built exquisitely beautiful harps in his business called Harps of Lorien. Today he also leads a variety of spiritual quests focused on caring for the planet and its resources, as well as guidance and direction for seekers.

ROBERT VAN ARSDALE – Robert was the primary architect and drafter of the plans and working drawings for the KMG Stupa. Preparing these documents was no easy feat as the design of a stupa is complex and far from ordinary. Robert had to draw the plans with sufficient detail and accuracy to obtain the required building permits and serve as the guide to the hands-on builders.

ANNE KIOUS – Anne was a quiet, steady worker on the building of the stupa. She was always smiling and encouraging without making a "fuss" about anything! She was also a smart accountant and shared her knowledge of budgeting and business operations on the stupa project. Anne has since passed away but remains forever in our hearts and our memories.

ANNA RUBYAN – Anna was a long-time and devoted student of Herman Rednick. She was a gifted musician and composer. She took many of the lyrics of poems that Herman had written and turned them into beautiful songs. Many of her songs and compositions are recorded and available in CD format. Anna passed away not long after the KMG stupa was completed, but she lives vibrantly on through her music and the memory of her angelic voice.

JANE LIPMAN – Jane is a long-time student of Herman Rednick and the group of students who follow his teachings. Jane helped with the building of the stupa and most generously, donated the land on which the stupa sits. In fact, she donated a total of five acres which permitted not only the building of the stupa but provided land for the building of a small kitchen and bathroom facilities. The land also now accommodates several retreat cabins that have been built on the property. Jane is a successful psychologist who also writes beautiful and meaningful poetry.

AL BARTH - Mr. Barth was a 94-year-old man who was like a father to me. He became great friends with Lama Dorje and they shared many delightful conversations. "Mr. B," as he was affectionately known, traveled to the KMG stupa site several times to view the work that was transpiring there. He was also an excellent cook and he was the one who prepared two large coolers filled with ribs that we grilled over an open fire for the visiting lamas the night before the consecration of the KMG stupa. He brought joy to the hearts of many.

In addition to those named, there were others who came by either serendipitously or by design as the stupa was being built and gave a hand for an afternoon or a day or two, folks like Joe Kanatser, Tsewang Tenzin and Patty Bott. I do not know the names of most of these people so I cannot include their names in this list. They know who they are and they know also how their lives have been blessed by the experience.

HAPPY 90th BIRTHDAY LAMA DORJE!

ABOUT THE AUTHOR

ALICE HERTER

Alice is a successful lawyer, architect and administrator. Raised in a traditional Christian home, her father's death when she was 18 years old propelled Alice on her spiritual journey. This journey included both the study of her own Christ-centered upbringing through Eastern religions and into Buddhism. In this book, Alice uses her talents to write the story of a Tibetan Buddhist monk whose wise and kind direction helped shape her spiritual life. His story is the story of a hero ... a man who relinquished worldly treasures and devoted his entire life to helping others. Alice brings his story to the reader in clear and concise language making the teachings readily accessible to all who read it.

Alice dedicates this book to her mother and expresses deep gratitude to all her family and friends who provided encouragement and support.

Printed in Great Britain
by Amazon

29284272R00137